Elite Soccer Drills

MICHAEL J. MATKOVICH

with

JASON DAVIS

Human Kinetics

Library of Congress Cataloging-In-Publication Data

Matkovich, Michael J.
  Elite soccer drills / Michael J. Matkovich with Jason Davis.
    p. cm.
  ISBN-13: 978-0-7360-7386-8 (soft cover)
  ISBN-10: 0-7360-7386-8 (soft cover)
  1. Soccer--Training. I. Davis, Jason, 1973- II. Title.

  GV943.9.T7M315 2009
  796.334--dc22

                        2008035438

  ISBN-10: 0-7360-7386-8
  ISBN-13: 978-0-7360-7386-8

Acquisitions Editor: Tom Heine; **Developmental Editor:** Anne Hall; **Assistant Editor:** Cory Weber; **Copyeditor:** Patsy Fortney; **Proofreader:** Coree Clark; **Graphic Designer:** Robert Reuther; **Graphic Artist:** Kim McFarland; **Cover Designer:** Keith Blomberg; **Photographer (cover):** Phil Cole/Getty Images; **Photographer (interior):** Neil Bernstein; **Photo Asset Manager:** Laura Fitch; **Visual Production Assistant:** Joyce Brumfield; **Photo Office Assistant:** Jason Allen; **Art Manager:** Kelly Hendren; **Associate Art Manager:** Alan L. Wilborn; **Illustrator:** Tim Brummett; **Printer:** United Graphics

We thank the Ultimate Soccer Arenas in Pontiac, Michigan, for assistance in providing the location for the photo shoot for this book.

Human Kinetics books are available at special discounts for bulk purchase. Special editions or book excerpts can also be created to specification. For details, contact the Special Sales Manager at Human Kinetics.

Printed in the United States of America   10 9   8   7   6   5   4   3   2   1

Human Kinetics
Web site: www.HumanKinetics.com

United States: Human Kinetics
P.O. Box 5076
Champaign, IL 61825-5076
800-747-4457
e-mail: humank@hkusa.com

Canada: Human Kinetics
475 Devonshire Road Unit 100
Windsor, ON N8Y 2L5
800-465-7301 (in Canada only)
e-mail: info@hkcanada.com

Europe: Human Kinetics
107 Bradford Road
Stanningley
Leeds LS28 6AT, United Kingdom
+44 (0) 113 255 5665
e-mail: hk@hkeurope.com

Australia: Human Kinetics
57A Price Avenue
Lower Mitcham, South Australia 5062
08 8372 0999
e-mail: info@hkaustralia.com

New Zealand: Human Kinetics
Division of Sports Distributors NZ Ltd.
P.O. Box 300 226 Albany
North Shore City
Auckland
0064 9 448 1207
e-mail: info@humankinetics.co.nz

Elite
Soccer Drills

Mike Matkovich: *For Dad*

Jason Davis: *For Kim, Jacob, Dylan, Mom, and Tim*

Contents

Drill Finder

Drill #	Drill Title	Page	NUMBER OF PLAYERS			Goal scoring	Maintaining possession	Offense/Defense/Both	Fitness building
			Individual	Small group	Large Group				
CHAPTER 2: SPEED, AGILITY, AND COORDINATION									
1	Acceleration	9	X	X	X				X
2	Agility Ladder Work	10	X	X	X				X
3	Stride Patterns	12	X	X	X				X
4	Agility Running 1	14	X	X	X				X
5	Agility Running 2	15	X	X	X				X
6	Agility Running 3	16	X	X	X				X
7	Jumping Patterns	18	X	X	X				X
8	Sprint Work With a Ball	20	X	X	X				X
9	Competitive Agility Training	22	X	X	X				X
10	Agility Hurdles	24	X	X	X				X
11	Star Agility Station	26	X	X	X				X
CHAPTER 3: JUGGLING									
12	Keep-Away (5v2)	30		X	X		X	X	X
13	Individual Juggling: Around the World	32	X	X	X				
14	Individual Juggling: Pattern and Sequence	34	X	X	X				
15	Individual Juggling: Speed Juggling	35	X	X	X				
16	Two-Player Juggling	36		X	X				
17	Group Juggling	38		X	X				
18	Group Juggling Relay	40		X	X				X
19	Group Juggling: Elimination	41		X	X				
CHAPTER 4: DRIBBLING									
20	Slalom Dribbling	45	X	X	X				X
21	Two Lines	46	X	X	X				X
22	Retreat Dribbling	48	X	X	X				X

Drill #	Drill Title	Page	NUMBER OF PLAYERS			Goal scoring	Maintaining possession	Offense/ Defense/ Both	Fitness building
			Individual	Small group	Large Group				
23	Changing the Dribbling Angle	50	X	X	X				X
24	Competitive 1v1 Dribbling 1	52		X	X		X	X	X
25	Competitive 1v1 Dribbling 2	54		X	X		X	X	X
26	1v1 Dribbling for Possession	55		X	X		X	X	X
27	Competitive Dribbling Games	56		X	X		X	X	X
28	Competitive Dribbling Games: Possession	58		X	X		X	X	X
29	Dribbling to Goal	59		X	X	X	X	X	X
30	The Gauntlet	60		X	X			X	X
CHAPTER 5: PASSING AND RECEIVING									
31	8v2	63			X		X	X	X
32	Two Lines	64		X	X				X
33	Groups of Four	66		X	X				X
34	Triangle Passing	68		X	X				X
35	Rectangle Passing	70		X	X				X
36	Four-Point Passing	72		X	X				X
37	4v2 (+2)	74		X	X		X	X	X
38	Passing Windows	76		X	X				X
39	Pairs	78		X	X		X	X	X
40	Groups of Three	80		X	X		X	X	X
41	Windows	82		X	X				X
42	Angle Passing and Receiving	84		X	X				X
43	Partners	86		X	X				X
44	Pattern Passing	88		X	X				X
45	Circle	90		X	X				X
CHAPTER 6: HEADING									
46	Head Passing	96		X	X				X
47	Up-and-Back Heading	98		X	X		X		X

(continued)

Foreword

Throughout my many years in the game of soccer, I have had the opportunity to observe and get to know many of the game's premier soccer coaches. In my opinion, Mike Matkovich is without question one of the best. Known as an outstanding teacher and trainer, Coach Matkovich has made a significant contribution to the growth and development of soccer in the United States.

His passion and knowledge of the game, along with his ability to teach the game of soccer to youth players, is the driving force behind his success.

As the director of the Chicago Magic Soccer Club, which is widely regarded as the top youth soccer club in America, he has spent countless hours teaching and molding young players and has helped to change the landscape of youth soccer. He has also shown his leadership in the pro arena by coaching two promising teams, Toronto FC in its inaugural year with the MLS, and Chivas USA. With Mike's assistance, both teams have garnered major victories in very quick succession in the major leagues.

The proof of his ability to teach is in his achievements and in his players. While at Indiana University, I had the privilege of working with a number of Coach Matkovich's former players, many of whom helped us win national championships and are now playing professionally.

I also competed against many of his former players. The two common threads among all of those players are their outstanding ability to execute the fundamentals of the game and their drive to be winners. I have no doubt that this comes directly from the time they spent under Coach Matkovich's guidance.

More recently, I have come to know Jason Davis as an outstanding coach and developer of youth talent. My teams at Indiana University competed against Jason while he was a player at the University of Akron, and in recent years we have recruited players that Jason has helped to produce.

Jason's innovative training ideas and talent for helping young soccer players develop into elite-level athletes is exemplified by the well-designed activities assembled in this book.

The drills in this book will help serious athletes achieve an elite level of competition both as individual and team players. The chapters have drills designed for individuals looking to hone their skills outside of team practice as well as activities designed for coaches who want to finesse their teams' prowess on the field. It is my privilege to endorse Matkovich and Davis' *Elite Soccer Drills*, and I highly recommend the book to anyone who is serious about reaching a new level.

Jerry Yeagley
All-time winningest coach, NCAA Div-I
National Soccer Hall of Fame Coach

Preface

Ten thousand hours. That is how many hours of training the experts say it takes to become an elite-level athlete in any sport. Soccer is no different. What the experts fail to mention, however, is that those ten thousand hours of training must take place in the correct environment, with the correct conditions, drills, supervision, and motivation.

This book provides information to help you create the elite environment your players need to accomplish their goals. It includes many of the drills, activities, and philosophies I have used to help players become successful at the individual and team level over the past 20 years. Whether your players want to make a club, high school, or college team, or the Olympic Development Program, the information in this book is invaluable.

Each chapter in *Elite Soccer Drills* is devoted to a core area of the game. The importance of setting high training standards and routines is covered in chapter 1, as is the importance of improving players' overall technical levels through self-training and small-group training. By focusing on small groups of one to four players, and then expanding the numbers when appropriate, you can focus on individual players.

Chapter 2 focuses on speed, agility, and coordination, the core components of a player's ability. At all levels, the ability to jump, sprint, and change directions quickly is essential to success. This chapter includes exercises that will help develop your speed, quickness, agility, and coordination, in a way that is very soccer specific. The exercises can be done individually or with a group, and can be adjusted according to the level of difficulty needed. Additionally, please note that throughout the drill chapters (chapters 2-9), the unit of distance given is yards. International readers who use the metric system can substitute the same distance in meters. For example, if the instructions use a distance of 20 yards, use 20 meters instead.

The focus of chapter 3 is juggling and how a regular juggling routine can help players' overall ability with the ball. The chapter includes juggling drills for one to five players and discusses ways to make juggling, alone or in a small group, competitive. Variations address the use of various body parts and the height, distance, and spin of the ball.

The focus of chapter 4 is dribbling. While the ability to dribble is one of the most basic skills a player has, it is often one of the most overlooked skills when it comes to actual practice. Many times, especially at younger ages (8-14), a coach will choose to focus on "team play" and passing, and sacrifices individual dribbling development in training. Chapter 4 is full of exercises that will help players develop and refine their individual dribbling skills and ball control. These exercises will help players improve their ability to beat defenders off the dribble, dribble to retain possession, and dribble to create space.

Passing and receiving are covered in chapter 5. Short, midrange, long, driven, and lofted passes are described and diagrammed. The chapter also includes drills that improve the mechanics and technique required for executing these skills.

The ability to head the ball effectively, with skill and purpose, is something that players often lack. Chapter 6 focuses exclusively on how to develop the ability to head the ball. The exercises in the chapter will help players with defensive heading, attacking heading (to goal), and with using heading to pass to a teammate.

Chapter 7 helps players improve the tactical side of the game by practicing small- and large-group attacking and defending. On the attacking side of the ball, 1v1, 2v2, 3v2, and 3v3 tactical situations are covered in great detail. Defending in similar situations, as well as improving players' ability to read the game and anticipate the play, are also described in chapter 7.

Chapter 8 outlines the techniques, mechanics, and drills for the final and most crucial phases of play: crossing and finishing. Methods for improving those areas through self-training and multiple-player training are detailed.

The final chapter is devoted to conditioning. From agility and quickness to aerobic and anaerobic fitness, all areas of fitness applied to soccer are covered. The chapter includes drills for agility and quickness training with and without the ball, along with drills for endurance and speed training. Finally, a number of fitness tests, and proper standards for each, are described.

The desire for self-improvement, on and off the field, is critical to success. However, only by knowing how to apply the correct methods and techniques, and by understanding the subtle nuances, can real development occur. We have used the methods and philosophies in this book to elevate teams and players to the highest youth and professional levels in the United States. By utilizing the exercises in this book you will have a great chance of reaching your goals, whether they are to make your high school team, play in college, or make it to the professional level.

Acknowledgments

We would like to acknowledge the following people who have contributed, directly and indirectly, to the content of this book and to our development as people and as coaches: Brett Hall, Jim Launder, Tim Carter, Alex Hernandez, David Richardson, Leo Ley, Dudley Duplee, Ken Lolla, Wayne Jentas, David Linenberger, Simon Spelling, Robert Davis, Tony Hermiz, Don Gemmell, Romero Aja, and Brett Jacobs.

Key to Diagrams

A	Attacker/Team A player		T	Target
B	Team B player		X	Player (general use)
C	Coach		Z	Team Z player
D	Defender		⌐•	Agility pole/flag
GK	Goalkeeper		⊢⊣	Agility hurdle
L	Left foot		△	Cone
N	Neutral player		⊛	Soccer ball
O	Opponent (general use)		----➤	Path of ball
R	Right foot		——➤	Path of player
S	Server		∿∿➤	Path of player dribbling ball

chapter 1

Becoming an Elite Player

Elite soccer players can be defined in a variety of ways. They are players with great skill, great pace and quickness, great strength, and great intelligence. One component, however, is often overlooked by both players and coaches: mentality. The mentality of elite athletes, soccer or otherwise, is unique.

Thousands of talented players have failed to maximize their potential for the simple reason that they were not mentally strong enough. So many players who have had skill, strength, and speed in abundance have failed. Why? Mentality.

The road to becoming an elite player is long and difficult. To make it to the top, players must be willing to make sacrifices. Missing out on social events, school events, and even family events is common among those who make it. Elite players accept such sacrifices as necessary.

Along the road, players may be told they are not good enough, smart enough, or fast enough. They may be cut from teams, lose their starting positions, or have long-term injuries. The need for the mental capacity to overcome such setbacks and challenges cannot be overstated. Elite players thrive on these types of challenges.

Elite players must be motivated to improve constantly. Fine-tuning and improving technical ability as well as physical ability are essential in the quest to become an elite player. The motivation to improve in all areas of the game must come from the players themselves.

Motivation

Parents frequently say, "Training is just not the same without someone giving instruction" or "Jamie doesn't work as hard when the coach is not there." Although there is likely some truth in such comments, the real issue is whether the player is motivated extrinsically or intrinsically. The difference is crucial.

Extrinsic motivation is based on external factors and tangible rewards. Although important and effective, extrinsic motivation is often shortsighted because it focuses exclusively on the reward, not the action. Once attained, the reward is gone. Intrinsic motivation comes from within. The person gets enjoyment from the activity or wants to push himself or improve beyond what he has already accomplished. Intrinsic motivation has a long-term payoff: As long as the person wants to better himself, the reward is always out there.

Clearly, to maximize ability, a player needs a combination of extrinsic and intrinsic motivation. However, only with a high degree of intrinsic motivation will that player reach her potential and make it to the highest levels of the game.

What to Focus On

Clearly, technique is the most important factor in a player's ability to play at a high level. Therefore, in small groups the main focus should be on improving players' overall technical ability, the ability to manipulate and control the ball under pressure.

Cristiano Ronaldo, who currently plays for Manchester United, is a great example of a player with such focus. He spends hours after training working exclusively on his ability with the ball. His hard work has clearly payed off; he is recognized as one of the most technically gifted players in the world.

In addition to technical skills, a player needs focus. The ability to grasp, understand, and react quickly to changes during a game can be the difference between winning and losing. When playing defense in a dead-ball situation, for example, the slightest lapse in concentration can be the difference between conceding a goal and preventing a goal. A lack of focus in a player defending a corner kick can lead to an opposing player getting free, having a scoring chance, and changing the game.

Unfortunately, parents and coaches in many sports still approach training with an attitude best characterized as "peaking by Friday." A short-term approach is taken to training and performance with an overemphasis on immediate results. We now know that a long-term commitment to practice and training is required for producing elite players and athletes in all sports.

Concentration, focus, and attitude are critical for success.

Any teacher, coach, or mentor will say that the training players do on their own is as, or more, important than organized team training. Developing a regular training routine to improve individual ability is crucial to players' development. Stories of David Beckham staying for hours after training to practice his free kicks while at Manchester United are legendary. The list of world-class players, including Beckham, Cristiano Ronaldo, Pelé, and Maradona, who religiously train on their own is too long to mention. If such training is good enough for the best players in the world, it is good enough for your players too.

Scientific research has concluded that it takes 8 to 12 years of training for a player to reach elite levels. This is called the 10-year rule, or 10,000-hour rule, which translates to slightly more than three hours of practice daily for 10 years.

Both time and economic constraints make meeting the rule nearly impossible if the only training a player does is with the team. Only by developing and maintaining a daily training routine, which focuses on the player's ability with the ball, will the player's ability improve enough to meet the technical demands of the highest levels.

Examples of Training Schedules

The following tables show two examples of how to organize a week to maximize time and training opportunities. Table 1.1 varies the focus each day so that a wide range of skills can be touched on, while table 1.2 maintains a focus on two skills for the entire week. These are simply examples and can be altered to meet the needs of individual players.

There is no right way to set up a training schedule. The focus will depend on the number of players participating in the training. Because the number of players involved in each self-training session fluctuates, players need to be flexible. If a player finds herself in a group of four players on a day when she planned to focus on dribbling, it would make sense to use all of the players and work on 1v1 or 2v2 attacking or defending principles.

The most important aspect of self-training is developing a routine. Only over time will a player make drastic improvements in ability level. Self-training is a crucial part of that. Developing a routine is not easy. The first step is setting achievable goals. Goals can be either specific (e.g., being able to juggle the ball 1,000 times by the end of the season) or broad (e.g., training outside of team practice three times per week).

Setting goals to focus on will help keep players focused and energized. At times they will have difficulty keeping up with their routines, such as in bad weather or when a field is closed or being used. Finding unique ways to keep up with their routines is essential. For example, when it is not possible

TABLE 1.1

Sunday	Monday	Tuesday	Wednesday	Thursday	Friday	Saturday
Self-train *Focus:* Playing 1v1 or 2v2 *Time:* 60 minutes	**Self-train** *Focus:* Juggling and long passing *Time:* 30 minutes	**Team/Club training**	**Self-train** *Focus:* Ball control and Agility *Time:* 60 minutes	**Team/Club training**	**Self-train** *Focus:* Juggling and dribbling *Time:* 45 minutes	**Team/Club matches**

TABLE 1.2

Sunday	Monday	Tuesday	Wednesday	Thursday	Friday	Saturday
Self-train *Focus:* Juggling and dribbling *Time:* 30 minutes	**Self-train** *Focus:* Juggling and dribbling *Time:* 30 minutes	**Team/Club training** **Self-train** *Focus:* Juggling and dribbling *Time:* 30 minutes	**Self-train** *Focus:* Juggling and dribbling *Time:* 30 minutes	**Team/Club training**	**Self-train** *Focus:* Juggling and dribbling *Time:* 30 minutes	**Team/Club matches**

to train on a field, a player can work on foot skills and technical ability on a racquetball court. Gymnasiums, basements, and tennis courts are also great places to train.

Developing a slightly different training regimen for each type of facility can also help to maintain a training program. For example, a basement where space is limited is ideal for practicing fast footwork with or without the ball. A racquetball court can help a player learn to react quickly and improve his ability to receive the ball.

Having the discipline and drive to develop and adhere to a training routine helps a player improve, and it sets the foundation, establishes the standard, and drives the team and its players to achieve progress and success.

chapter 2

Speed, Agility, and Coordination

Over the past decade, speed, agility, and coordination (SAC) training has become an important component in the development of elite soccer players. At all levels of the game—youth, amateur, and professional—SAC training helps players develop or refine key physical abilities.

SAC training generally focuses on short bursts of running, jumping, and hopping and includes quick changes of direction; patterned footwork around poles, cones, and ladders; and isolated technical training with a ball.

For the youngest players, SAC training is used for macro purposes: to help young players develop better balance, coordination, and overall body awareness and control. The training includes all parts of the body and incorporates a lot of jumping, tumbling, and rolling. The goal with the youngest players is to help them improve their body awareness. Learning how to balance the body when jumping or hopping, as well as learning how to fall, roll, and tumble, is crucial to developing athletic ability.

The elite youth and professional levels use SAC training to isolate specific aspects of the player's physical development. By focusing on the quality, rather than quantity, of repetition, elite coaches use SAC training to improve running technique, balance, acceleration, foot speed, and technique in a soccer-specific setting.

Duration and Equipment

SAC training should be done at the beginning of training sessions when players are fresh and can focus on the quality of their performance without being hindered by muscle fatigue. Also, there is less risk of soft tissue injuries when players are fresh and muscles are not fatigued. SAC training can also be used, to a lesser extent, as a warm-up before matches. A warm-up consisting of two to four SAC exercises is a dynamic way to help players prepare for a match.

The most common format used in SAC training is a circuit course. Setting up five to eight stations and allowing small groups to go through each station for a set time, usually two to four minutes per station, allow each player the opportunity to get a complete SAC workout.

Certain training equipment is helpful for setting up SAC training. The basics include cones, plastic rods or poles, agility rings, agility ladders, and hurdles. More advanced equipment, usually found at colleges and professional clubs, includes running sleds, running parachutes, agility boxes, speed bands, heart rate monitors, and timing equipment. For the purposes of this book, we focus only on drills that are done with basic equipment. Many coaches who do not have access to, or the budget for, agility poles, agility ladders, and other equipment often find unique and inexpensive ways to create their own equipment—for example, using PVC piping in place of agility poles, or using cones or a rope to make an agility ladder.

The following pages present SAC exercises and ideas that can be combined in a variety of ways to create circuit courses for your players. Some basic considerations are necessary when creating a circuit course. First, are you using the circuit as a warm-up, a main component of practice, or a cool-down? Warm-up and cool-down circuits should not be overly demanding physically, whereas circuits used in the middle of training sessions should be physically taxing.

Next, overloading on one type of exercise, such as jumping or sprinting, is not recommended because it can cause players to become overly fatigued and injured. Having a good balance among three or four types of exercises, and varying the order, is a good starting point.

Finally, consider the duration at each station, as well as the amount of rest between stations. Generally, spending two to three minutes per station is a good starting point, and one to three minutes of rest between stations is a good ratio.

ACCELERATION

Purpose

Improve balance, acceleration, and speed.

Organization

Using four cones or poles, make a diamond with 1-yard sides. Place a fifth and sixth cone 10 yards in front of the diamond, with 5 yards between them, creating a finish line. Groups of 5 to 10 players stand in a line behind the southernmost cone. Each player performs the activity and then walks to the end of the line.

Procedure

The first player starts in the center of the diamond with his feet together. In quick succession, he jumps with feet together over the cone or pole to his left, back to the center, over the cone or pole to his right, back to the center, and then runs to the cone 10 yards in front of him.

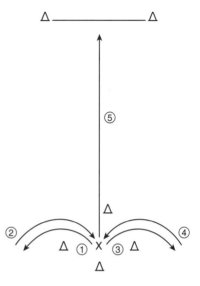

Key Points

- Keep your feet together.
- Use your arms to help balance.
- Land on the front part of the foot.
- Accelerate using the front part of the foot.

Variations

1. Players perform jumps with their backs to the finishing cone, then turn and run facing forward.

2. Players hop on one foot over the left cone, back to center, over the right cone, back to center, and then run forward. Repeat using opposite foot.

3. Players roll, tumble, or perform a header while running to the finishing line.

4. Each player performs a technical action at the finishing line. Technical actions could include passing to a designated player or taking a goal shot.

5. Each player receives the ball from a server (a designated player standing 10 yards past the finish line) and performs a technical action—volley, header, goal shot—at the finish line, then passes the ball back to the server.

Purpose

Improve balance, foot speed, and foot coordination.

Organization

Secure an agility ladder to the ground or floor. Groups of five to seven players form a line at one end of the ladder. Players go through the ladder performing specific exercises, then walk to the end of the line.

Procedure

The player steps to the left and just in front of the first rung of the ladder and goes through the ladder performing the following pattern: right foot inside, left foot inside, right foot outside, left foot inside, right foot inside, left foot outside, right foot inside, left foot inside, and so on (a).

Key Points

- Concentrate on the correct pattern before speed.
- Use your arms to help balance.
- Increase foot speed as the pattern becomes easier to perform.

Variations

1. Players go through the same pattern, except backward.
2. Players jump with two feet over the rungs of the ladder.
3. Players hop on one foot over the rungs of the ladder.
4. Players step over, step back, jump over, and then jump and hop over rungs of ladder (one and two footed). The players can perform the activity facing forward or backward. They go through the entire ladder hopping on two feet, then go through hopping on the right foot only, then on the left foot only.
5. Players run through the ladder, lift their knees high, and allow both feet to touch the ground between each rung as they go through.
6. Players move along either side of the ladder in a right-foot-in, left-foot-in, right-foot-out, left-foot-out, right-foot-in, left-foot-in pattern—two in, two out (forward and back).
7. Players start on the right side of the ladder and move through the ladder in a zigzag, right-foot-in, left-foot-in, right-foot-out, left-foot-out, right-foot-in, right-foot-in pattern—two in, two out (b).

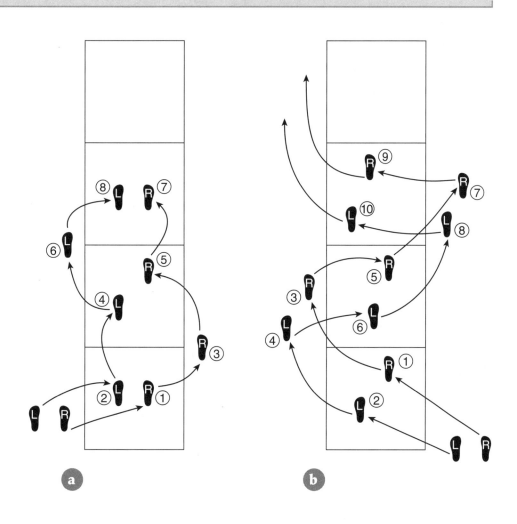

3   STRIDE PATTERNS

Purpose

Improve foot speed, foot coordination, and acceleration.

Organization

Place 8 to 10 agility poles parallel in a row, and increase the spacing between each pole gradually. The pole spacing should start at 1 foot (30 cm) and gradually increase to 2 yards. Place a cone 2 yards behind the first pole to mark the starting point.

Procedure

Players start behind the cone. At your signal, the first player runs over the poles, making sure to adjust her stride length as she goes over each pole. Upon reaching the last pole, she should be running at speed, with long strides, and finish with a 10-yard sprint. Each player performs 5 to 10 repetitions (a).

Key Points

- Concentrate on organizing your feet before going for speed.
- Use your arms to help balance.
- Increase foot speed as the pattern becomes easier to perform.

Variations

1. Rather than gradually increasing the distance between the poles, vary the distance from short to long so the players have to speed up and slow down as they go over the poles.

2. Add a technical action at the end of the sprint:
    a. Header
    b. Pass
    c. Volley
    d. Shot (b)
    e. Cross (c)
    f. Any combination of techniques

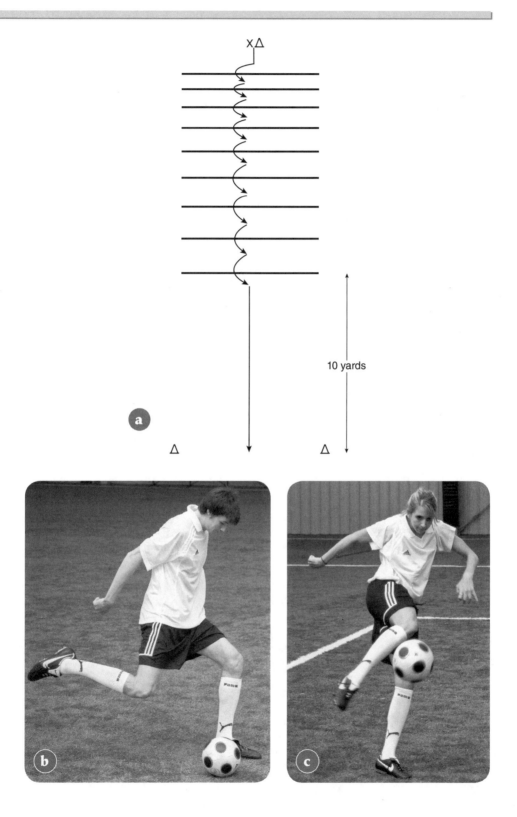

X△

10 yards

a

△   △

b

c

AGILITY RUNNING 1

Purpose

Improve balance, foot speed, and foot coordination.

Organization

Place cones to form a 30- × 15-yard rectangle. The cones that form the center slalom should be 1 yard apart.

Procedure

At your signal, the player at cone A runs at top speed to cone B, then back to the opposite side, followed by a slalom up and back through the center cones and then back up to cone C. The player proceeds to cone D for the finish.

Key Points

- Concentrate on the correct pattern before speed.
- Use your arms to help balance.
- Shorten your stride length when changing direction.

Variations

1. Increase the distances between the cones.
2. Players run backward through the course.
3. Players perform technical actions at any or all of points A, B, and C.
4. Time each run and mark players' progress.

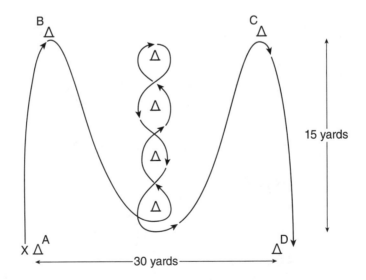

AGILITY RUNNING 2

Purpose
Improve balance, foot speed, and foot coordination.

Organization
Set cones in a Y formation to be used as a guide for the players. Players proceed through the course and trace the Y cone pattern.

Procedure
At your signal, the player runs through the course as quickly as possible. The player starts at the center cone and runs around the cone to her right, going in a counterclockwise direction.

Key Points
- Concentrate on the correct pattern before speed.
- Use your arms to help balance.
- Shorten your stride length when changing direction.

Variations
1. Increase the distances.
2. Players run backward through the entire course.
3. Players run through the course facing the same direction throughout, so they are running backward for sections A, B, and C.
4. Time each run and mark players' progress.

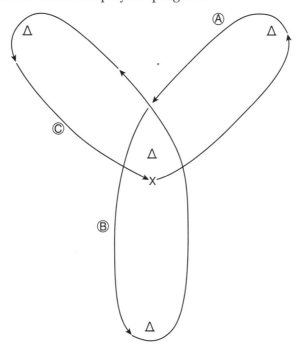

AGILITY RUNNING 3

Purpose

Improve balance, foot speed, and foot coordination.

Organization

Place six cones in an indented triangle pattern; players perform actions between the cones.

Procedure

At your signal, the player runs through the course as quickly as possible. When shuffling in sections B and C, the player moves sideways without letting his feet cross. Incorporate the actions listed in the diagram that correspond to points A through F.

Key Points

- Concentrate on the correct pattern before speed.
- Use your arms to help balance.
- Shorten your stride length when changing direction.

Variations

1. Increase the distances.
2. Players run backward through the entire course.
3. Time each run and mark players' progress.

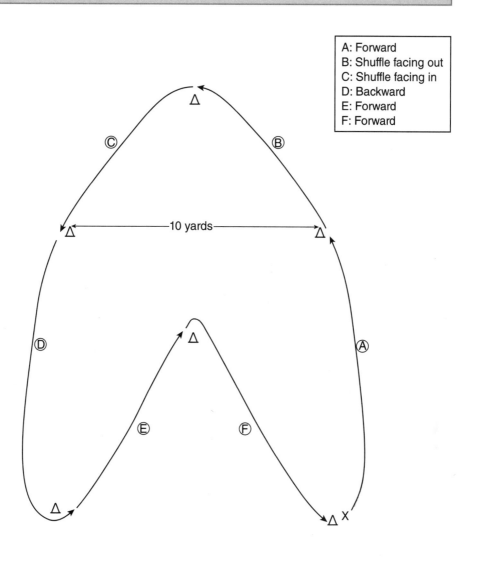

A: Forward
B: Shuffle facing out
C: Shuffle facing in
D: Backward
E: Forward
F: Forward

10 yards

7   JUMPING PATTERNS

Purpose

Improve balance, jumping ability, and coordination.

Organization

Using poles, set up four to six jumping gates, all at mid-shin height. In variations 1 and 2, the height varies.

Procedure

At your signal, the player runs through the course as quickly as possible, jumping over each gate (a). The player should keep both feet together and bring his knees up when jumping. Players hurdle over the higher gates used in the variations. Players can jump over hurdles or gates with both feet together or one foot at a time.

Key Points

- Organize your feet before jumping.
- Use your arms to help balance.
- Shorten your stride length when approaching the gate.

Variations

1. Vary the height of the gates so that they get gradually higher. Random variation of the height is also useful.
2. Adjust the gates' heights alternately so that players must jump over the first gate, duck or roll under the second, jump over the third, duck or roll under the fourth, and so on (b).
3. Time each run and mark players' progress.
4. Add a technical action, such as a pass or heading the ball to a designated player at the end of the course.
5. Using only one gate, players touch the ball under the gate, then jump over the gate, collect the ball, and end with a shot on goal, a cross, or a pass.
6. Using only one gate, for 30 seconds, players pass the ball under the gate, jump over the gate, collect the ball, pass the ball back under the gate in the reverse direction, jump over the gate, collect the ball, and repeat.

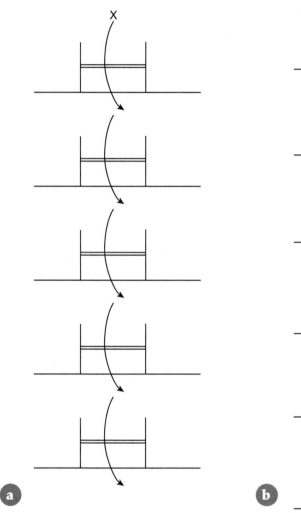

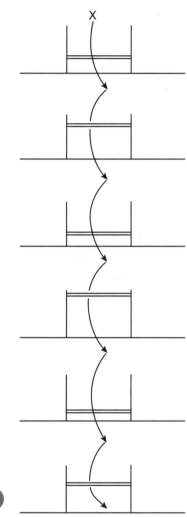

SPRINT WORK WITH A BALL

Purpose

Improve foot speed, acceleration, and technical ability while running.

Organization

Mark a 20-yard line and separate it into 5-yard intervals using cones. Place one ball at each of the 5- and 10-yard markers. Place servers on the right and left of the 15-yard line.

Procedure

At your signal, player 1 sprints out to the 5-yard marker, collects the ball, and dribbles back to the starting point. She then turns and sprints out to the 10-yard marker and plays the ball to the receiving player 15 yards away and sprints back to the starting point. She then sprints out to the 15-yard marker. As player 1 approaches the marker, server 1 plays the ball into player 1's path, at which point player 1 shoots at goal and then sprints back to the starting point. Finally, player 1 sprints out to the 20-yard marker, turns, collects a pass from server 2, and dribbles back to the starting point to finish (a).

Key Points

- Shorten your stride when changing direction.
- Adjust your feet in order to receive balls with a good first touch.

Variations

1. Increase the distances for more fitness.
2. Server 1 throws the ball for player 1 to volley at goal.
3. After receiving the ball from server 2, player 1 turns and dribbles to goal, ending with a shot (b).
4. Each time player 1 returns to the starting point, she performs a technical action:
    a. Volley
    b. Header
    c. Pass
    d. Shot
5. Time each run and mark players' progress.

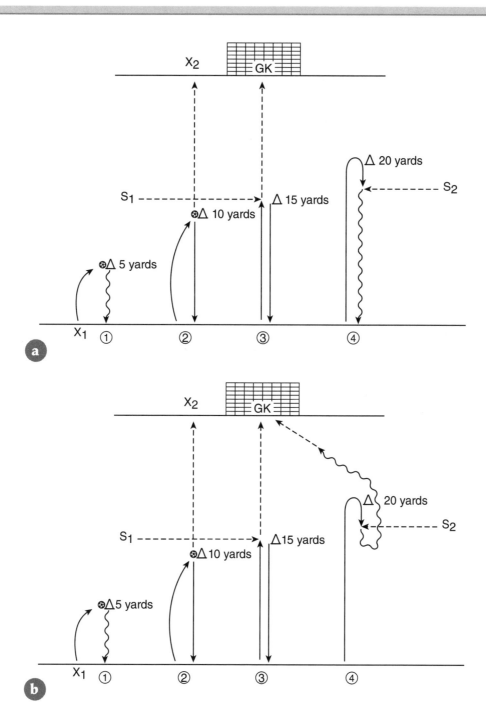

COMPETITIVE AGILITY TRAINING

Purpose

Improve balance, foot speed, and foot coordination.

Organization

Set out two sets of agility poles in a slalom pattern, side by side. Mark a finish line clearly with cones 10 yards past the last pole.

Procedure

At your signal, players 1 and 2 slalom through the agility poles, then turn and sprint back to the starting point, touching the line with their feet. They then sprint to the finish line (a).

Key Points

- Use quick feet through slalom poles.
- Shorten your stride length when changing direction.

Variations

1. Increase the finish line distance.
2. Players run backward through the course.
3. Players dribble a ball across the finish line.
4. Add a second set of agility poles, forcing players to sprint between sets (b).
5. Rather than sprinting or dribbling a ball each across the finish line, the players race to one ball, and then attack goal, with player 1 attacking and player 2 defending.
6. Time each run and mark players' progress.

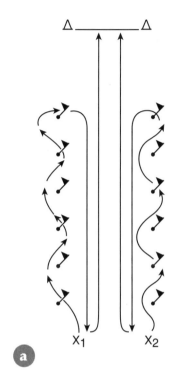

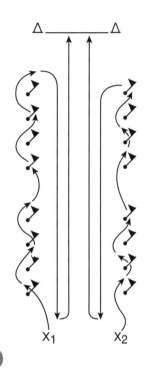

10   AGILITY HURDLES

Purpose
Improve balance, foot speed, and foot coordination.

Organization
Lay out 8 to 10 stand-alone agility hurdles in a row. Mark a starting point with a cone.

Procedure
At your signal, the player runs over the hurdles as quickly as possible, touching both feet in the space between each set of hurdles.

Key Points
- Concentrate on the correct pattern before speed.
- Use your arms to help balance.
- Raise your knees when running.
- Move your arms in unison with your legs.

Variations
1. Players add a sprint at the end of the row.
2. Players run backward through the course.
3. Players perform a technical action at the end of the row:
   a. Volley
   b. Shot
   c. Pass
   d. Cross
   e. Dribble
   f. Header
4. Players hop or jump over hurdles, rather than running:
   a. With both feet together
   b. Left foot only
   c. Right foot only
   d. With both feet together, raising knees as high as possible
5. Players run over hurdles sideways, touching both feet in the space between each set of hurdles.
   a. Lead with right side.
   b. Lead with left side.
6. Lay hurdles out in a random direction. Players must face the same direction while hopping over each hurdle.
7. Time each run and mark players' progress.

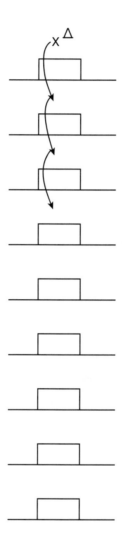

11

STAR AGILITY STATION

Purpose

Improve balance, foot speed, and foot coordination.

Organization

Place cones in a cross formation, with each outer cone 10 yards from the center cone *(a)*.

Procedure

At your signal, the player does the following:

1. Sprints forward to center
2. Shuffles to the right
3. Shuffles back to center
4. Sprints forward
5. Sprints backward to center
6. Shuffles to the left
7. Shuffles back to center
8. Sprints backward to the end

Key Points

- Use your arms to help balance.
- Shorten your stride length when changing direction.

Variations

1. Increase the distances.
2. Players perform technical actions at various points.
   a. Volley
   b. Pass
   c. Header
3. Add cones A, B, C, and D. Players complete the eight actions listed above and sprint forward out and backward back at the additional cones as well *(b)*.
4. Time each run and mark players' progress.

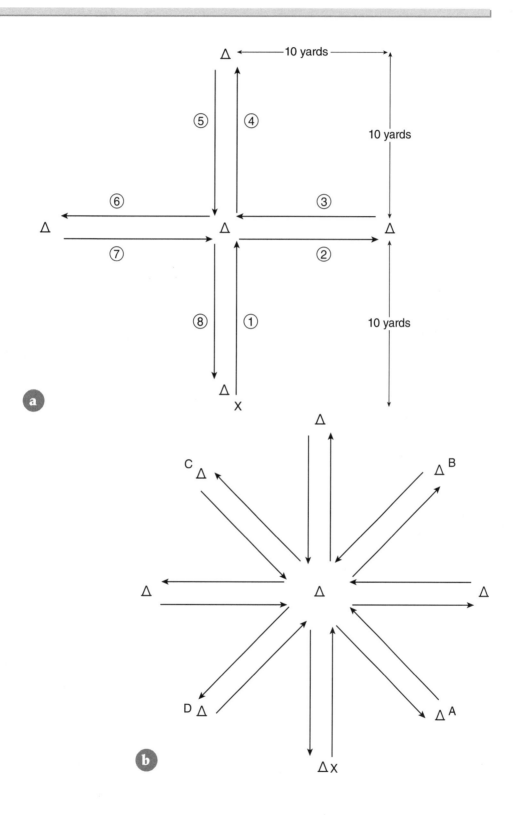

chapter 3

Juggling

You don't often see a player in a high-level match collect a ball and juggle it down the field past opponents. However, the ability to juggle the ball has a direct correlation to the ability to control the ball. Therefore, it is vital to players' development that they make juggling a part of their training routines.

Juggling instills a sense of discipline and work ethic in players. Only through repetition and practice will players see improvement. At first, juggling is not easy, and it is frustrating. But with a commitment to improving, players can improve their juggling ability and their ability to control the ball.

Juggling also gives players a sense of how to use nearly every part of the body to control and manipulate the ball. The chest, knees, thighs, shoulders, shins, feet, heels, and back are all in play when juggling. Generally, players are most comfortable learning to juggle with their thighs, likely because they have the most surface area to strike the ball. However, it is highly recommended that players learn to juggle with their feet first. Although this is initially more difficult, improving timing and touch with the feet is the foundation for improvement.

In addition to improving players' feel for the ball, juggling improves timing and overall coordination in relation to the ball. Because players are constantly adjusting to the height and spin of the ball, footwork and balance improve naturally. Striking the ball at different heights varies not only the degree of difficulty in keeping the ball in the air but also the degree of difficulty in maintaining balance. Learning muscle group control is essential as players move through the higher levels of the game. The better control players have, the less energy they expend when in possession of the ball.

The number of juggling variations is virtually limitless. The following pages provide a variety of juggling activities that will improve players' juggling ability, ball control, footwork, balance, body control, and overall coordination.

12

KEEP-AWAY (5V2)

Purpose

Improve the overall ability to control flighted balls.

Organization

Groups of 7 to 10 players form a small circle with 2 players holding colored training bibs in the middle, to indentify them as defenders.

Procedure

Player 1 serves the ball with the hands to player 2, who must juggle the ball, then pass it in the air to another player, without the two defending players (D1 and D2) in the middle stealing the ball (*a*).

If one of the defending players intercepts or touches the ball, or the ball hits the ground, the player who made the pass or dropped the ball replaces the defender who has been in the center the longest.

Defenders can steal the ball only when it is being passed between players.

Key Points

- Choose a controlling surface early.
- Judge the spin and pace of the pass early.
- Don't pass the ball until you are balanced.

Variations

1. Players allow the ball to bounce once between passes or touches.
2. Defenders must walk in the middle to make it slightly easier for the players on the outside of the circle to pass the ball to each other.
3. Limit the number of touches the outside players are allowed to take.
4. Do not allow headers.
5. Have players use one defender rather than two (*b*).

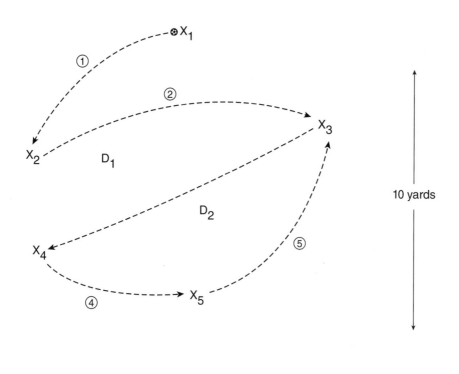

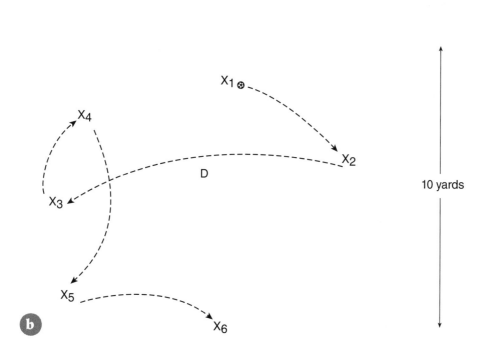

13   INDIVIDUAL JUGGLING: AROUND THE WORLD

Purpose
Improve the overall ability to control flighted balls.

Organization
One to 20 players, each with a ball and enough space to juggle the ball.

Procedure
At your signal, each player attempts to juggle the ball in the Around the World sequence: right foot, right thigh, right shoulder, head, left shoulder, left thigh, left foot, left thigh, left shoulder, head, right shoulder, right thigh, right foot (*a-c*). There is no time limit for beginners. For more advanced players, time limits can be used.

Key Points
- Judge the spin and pace of the ball early to decide how soft or hard to touch the ball as it comes down.
- Touch the ball high enough to get underneath it for the next touch.

Variations
1. Allow players to take as many touches as they like at each point in the sequence.
2. Players can catch the ball on the backs of their necks for a rest at the halfway point (pick a country).

14 INDIVIDUAL JUGGLING: PATTERN & SEQUENCE

Purpose

Improve the overall ability to control flighted balls.

Organization

One to 20 players, each with a ball and enough space to juggle the ball.

Procedure

At your signal, each player attempts to juggle the ball in a low-low-high, low-low-high sequence using any part of the body. *Low* and *high* refer to the height the ball is kicked or hit in the air after the player touches it. The greater the height, the more difficult the ball is to control. No time limit or penalties.

Key Points

- Judge the spin and pace of the ball early.
- Stay balanced.
- Test yourself by hitting the high ball a bit higher each time.

Variations

1. Allow players to bounce the ball between touches.
2. Here are other patterns:
    a. Right, left, right, left
    b. Foot, foot, thigh, thigh, head, head, foot, foot
    c. Right (once), left (once), right (twice), left (twice), right (three times), left (three times)
    d. Right foot or side only
    e. Left foot or side only

Purpose
Improve the overall ability to control flighted balls.

Organization
One to 20 players, each with a ball and enough space to juggle the ball.

Procedure
Set a timer for 30 seconds. On your signal, the players juggle as many times as possible in 30 seconds. Players who drop their balls should lift them again and continue counting.

Key Points
- Keep the ball as low as possible.
- Use the feet as much as possible.
- Judge the spin and pace of the ball early.
- Stay balanced.

Variations
1. Restrict which body parts players can use.
2. Increase the time (60 seconds).
3. If they drop the ball, players must start from zero again.
4. Players can use headers only.

Purpose

Improve the overall ability to control flighted balls.

Organization

One to 20 players, in pairs, with one ball per pair.

Procedure

Player 1 begins juggling while player 2 jogs backward 5 yards, then forward 5 yards to the starting point. Player 1 passes the ball in the air to player 2, who juggles while player 1 jogs backward and then forward. The players continue the pattern for a set time (*a*).

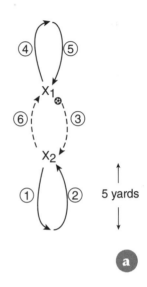

Key Points

- Judge the spin and pace of the ball early.
- Pass the ball to your partner with enough height that he can get underneath the ball (*b*).

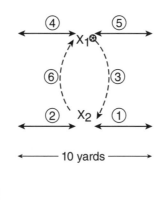

— 10 yards —

c

Variations

1. Restrict the number of touches each player can take when juggling.

2. Restrict or limit the parts of the body players can use.

3. Player 2 shuffles side to side 5 yards and then receives the ball *(c)*.

4. Player 2 jogs around player 1 while he is juggling. Player 1 passes the ball when player 2 gets back in front of him.

5. Players stand 5 yards apart, facing each other. After a set number of touches, player 1 pops the ball up in the air over player 2's head. Player 2 then turns and receives or continues juggling the ball back to player 1 and pops it over player 1's head for him to retrieve. The players continue the pattern for a set time.

6. Players 1 and 2 pass the ball back and forth, increasing the number of touches by one with each pass. For example: Player 1 serves, and with one touch player 2 touches the ball back to player 1. Player 1 receives the ball and touches it twice, passing it back to player 2 with the second touch. Player 2 takes three touches, passing it back to player 1 with the third touch. Player 1 takes four touches, passing it back to player 2 with the fourth touch, and so on.

17

GROUP JUGGLING

Purpose

Improve the overall ability to control flighted balls.

Organization

Groups of four players with one ball, separated by 10 yards into two lines of two players.

Procedure

Player 1 moves across to player 2 while juggling the ball. When she reaches player 2, she passes the ball in the air to player 2, who then juggles across to player 3, who receives the ball and will continue the pattern to player 4 (a). All passes should be made in the air. If the ball hits the ground, players should try to pass the ball off of the bounce, and not let the ball settle on the ground. Player 4 then returns the ball to player 1, starting the sequence again. The players repeat the pattern for a set time.

Key Points

- Move slowly across the line.
- Limit the spin from each touch.
- Serve the ball to the next player with enough height that she can take a good first touch.

Variations

1. Allow the ball to bounce between touches.
2. Player 1 serves the ball in the air to player 2, who controls or juggles the ball and then serves it in the air to player 3, who is standing behind player 1. Player 1 follows his pass across the line, switching to the other side. The players repeat the pattern for a set time (b).
3. Player 1 juggles the ball across. At the halfway point he plays the ball, in the air, to player 2, who plays it back to player 1 with one touch. Player 1 plays it back to player 2 with one touch, and player 2 juggles across to player 3 and repeats the passing pattern.

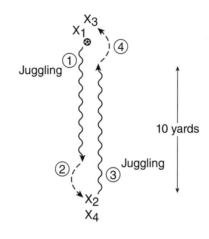

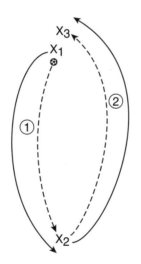

18

GROUP JUGGLING RELAY

Purpose

Improve the overall ability to control flighted balls.

Organization

Groups of four to six players, with one ball per group. Players stand in a line with the ball at the first player's feet. Place a cone 10 yards in front of the line.

Procedure

At your signal, player 1 juggles the ball out to the cone, turns, and passes the ball, in the air, back to player 2. Player 1 stays by the cone to be the receiver for the other players. The other players stay in line and do not run forward. Player 2 controls or juggles the ball, passes it back to player 1, and then goes to the end of the line. Player 1 controls or juggles the ball and passes it, in the air, to player 3, who controls it, plays it back to player 1, and goes to the end of the line. Players continue the pattern until player 2 receives the ball again. He then replaces player 1 at the cone, and the pattern is repeated until all players have been at the cone.

Key Points

- Judge the spin and pace of the ball early.
- Choose a controlling surface early.
- Pass the ball across only when you are balanced and have had a good preparatory touch.

Variations

1. Allow the ball to bounce between touches.
2. Restrict the parts of the body the players can use (e.g., feet only).
3. Increase or decrease the distance between the line and the cone based on the ability level of the players.

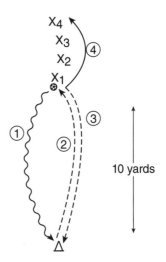

10 yards

Purpose

Improve the overall ability to control flighted balls.

Organization

Groups of three to seven players, with one ball per group.

Procedure

Player 1 serves the ball with her hands to player 2 and calls out a number between 1 and 5 while the ball is in the air. This is the number of touches player 2 should make in her juggling. Player 2 must control, juggle, and pass the ball to player 3 without letting it touch the ground. Player 3 repeats the pattern and moves the ball to player 4. If the ball is dropped or an unplayable pass is given, the player who dropped the ball or made the unplayable pass is eliminated. Eliminated players juggle on their own while the game finishes.

Key Points

- Judge the spin and pace of the ball early.
- Choose a controlling surface early.

Variations

1. Players serve with their hands.
2. Players serve with their feet—from a volley.
3. Players serve with their feet—from the ground.
4. Restrict the use of body parts (e.g., no headers).

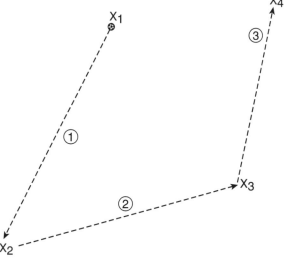
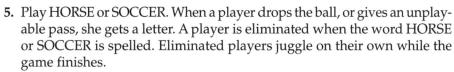

5. Play HORSE or SOCCER. When a player drops the ball, or gives an unplayable pass, she gets a letter. A player is eliminated when the word HORSE or SOCCER is spelled. Eliminated players juggle on their own while the game finishes.

chapter 4

Dribbling

Without question, dribbling is a key skill if a player is to succeed at the very highest level of the game. Though considered a basic skill, dribbling is the most dynamic and exciting component in the game.

Many think of dribbling as simply running with the ball. However, at the highest level of the game, dribbling is more than that; it is the ability to manipulate, control, and move the ball to gain or maintain an advantage. The best players in the world tend to use dribbling for three basic purposes: to beat or eliminate defenders by running past them with the ball, to create new passing lanes and angles, and to maintain possession and control of the ball. Players who use dribbling to good advantage to accomplish one or more of these purposes are often referred to as "having good feet."

Examples of players who use dribbling successfully to accomplish these three purposes are not difficult to find in today's game. Lionel Messi of Argentina and Brazil's Ronaldinho are two obvious examples of players who use dribbling moves to beat and eliminate defenders in order to create an advantage for their teams. The ability to combine dribbling, feints, and changes of pace makes these players two of the most creative, dynamic, and explosive attacking players in the world.

Speed dribbling is also used to eliminate defenders and to gain territory when attacking. Manchester United's Cristiano Ronaldo and Real Madrid's Arjen Robben are two of the best examples in soccer today of players who use dribbling at speed to create attacking advantages for their teams. The best speed dribblers have the ability to keep close control of the ball when running at close to top speed. By moving not only their bodies, but the ball as well, at a rapid rate, Ronaldo and Robben are able to unbalance their opponents and create space to run into.

Creating passing angles is crucial to creating scoring chances, and through creative and intelligent dribbling, players can create those angles. Often, moving the ball as little as two or three yards can create various attacking and possession options. Although many observers associate space, time, and speed with the option to dribble, the ability to manipulate and move the ball in a tight, pressurized space is dribbling in perhaps its most potent form.

Using a slight feint when a defender is approaching is a great way to cause the defender to slow down, lose balance, or both. Accelerating with the ball is an effective way to get away from a defender when there is open space behind the defender. In this situation, the attacking player can afford to have the ball farther from his body, allow him to touch the ball ahead and sprint to catch up to the ball.

French legend Zinedine Zidane and AC Milan and Brazilian attacking midfielder Kaká are two of the best exponents of dribbling with the ball in a tight area to create passing lanes. Zidane, in particular, had the unique ability to use a wide range of touches on the ball to move defenders into vulnerable positions and then exploit them with lethal passes. Using a variety of foot surfaces can help a player move the ball into a position in which the defender thinks she can steal it, baiting the defender into attempting the steal; the player then quickly moves the ball away from the defender and into open space.

Dribbling to beat players and to create passing angles requires players to actually move the ball in and out of pressure in order to maintain possession for their teams. By dribbling the ball sideways or backward, players can create time and space while reducing the amount of pressure placed on them by the opposing team.

All players, no matter their defensive or offensive positions, can use the skill of dribbling to work their way out of pressurized situations. For example, target forwards use dribbling under pressure to hold the ball in order to create time for their teammates to join the attack.

Although players use most, or almost all, of their body parts when dribbling, the feet are obviously the part most used. Many coaches in soccer today work on the principle that six surfaces of the foot are used when training to improve dribbling:

1. Top of the foot
2. Sole of the foot
3. Toe
4. Inside of the foot
5. Outside of the foot
6. Heel

Although that view is not wrong, it is far too simplistic and compartmentalized. When training players at or near the highest levels of the game, coaches should adopt the mind-set that effective dribbling requires the use of the whole foot and that every part of the dribbling foot can be used to the player's advantage.

The activities in this chapter isolate or combine the following dribbling objectives:

- Beat or eliminate defenders by running at and past them with ball.
- Create new passing lanes and angles.
- Maintain possession and control of the ball.

20 SLALOM DRIBBLING

Purpose
Improve overall ball control when dribbling, and improve foot speed and coordination.

Organization
Place 10 flags or cones in a line with 1 yard between each.

Procedure
Players move with the ball around the poles performing various dribbling patterns.

Key Point
The feet should be moving quickly, while the ball moves at a slower pace. You have to reorganize your feet while the ball is moving, so your feet are actually moving faster than the ball is rolling.

Variations
1. Players slalom around the poles using any part of both feet.
2. Players use right foot only.
3. Players use left foot only.
4. Players use both feet, inside only.
5. Players use both feet, outside only.
6. Pattern 1: Players dribble around the first pole with the inside of the right foot, stop the ball with the sole of the right foot, dribble around the next pole with the inside of the left foot, stop the ball with the sole of the left foot, and repeat. (Inside right, stop, inside left, stop, inside right, stop.)
7. Pattern 2: Players rake around the poles with inside of the right foot, stop with outside of the right foot, rake through the next poles with inside of the left foot, stop with outside of the left foot, repeat (rake, stop, rake, stop, rake, stop).

Purpose

Improve the ability to dribble to beat an opponent, and maintain overall ball control.

Organization

Create two lines, with three to six players in each line. Lines are 15 to 20 yards apart, with one flag or cone in the middle. For more repetitions, have several groups working at the same time.

Procedure

The first player from each line dribbles slowly toward the flag, then changes pace and accelerates to the opposite line.

Key Points

- Keep the ball close when dribbling slowly; then take a big touch to accelerate.
- Use the outside of the foot when preparing the ball for the bigger, accelerating touch.
- Keep the ball on the outside of your body when dribbling.
- Alternate feet.

Variations

1. Players switch the ball in the middle, then accelerate.
2. Inside-outside fake: Players slowly drag the ball across the body with the inside of the foot to unbalance their opponents, then quickly accelerate with an outside-of-the-foot touch to go past the opponent.
3. Double fake: Players slowly drag the ball across the body with the inside of the right foot, then, rather than taking the ball with the outside of the right foot, they step past the ball with the right foot and take it away with the outside of the left foot.
4. Inside-out step-over: Players bring the right foot around the back and inside of the ball, then take the ball away to the left, using the outside of the left foot.
5. Double step-over: Players bring the right foot around the back and inside of the ball, then, rather than taking it away with the outside of the left foot, they step over the back and inside of the ball with the left foot and take it away to the right with the outside of the right foot.

6. Outside-in step-over: With the right foot, players step around the outside and front of the ball, with the right foot landing on the inside of the ball. Then they take the ball away with the outside of the right foot.

7. Ronaldo rake: With the inside of the right foot, players rake (roll) the ball across the body, step over the outside and front of the ball with the left foot, and then take ball away to the left with the outside of the left foot.

Purpose

Improve the ability to turn and dribble away from pressure, and improve overall ball control.

Organization

Place four cones 20 yards apart in the form of a cross, with one flag in the center. Two players stand in a line outside each cone. Each player has a ball.

Procedure

The first player from each line dribbles to the center flag, turns using an outside-of-the-foot chop, and dribbles back to the starting cone. To perform the outside-of-the-foot chop, the player pushes the ball out in front of him, moves to retrieve it, and then uses the outside of his foot to cut the ball back toward the direction it came from.

Key Points

- Keep the ball close to the foot when performing the chop; then take a big touch with the outside of the foot to accelerate away.
- Perform using both feet.

Variations

1. Players use an inside-of-the-foot chop.
2. Players dribble out to the cone, stop the ball with the sole of the foot, step past the ball, and turn back toward the starting cone, taking a big touch to accelerate away.
3. To turn, players step over outside and in front of the ball with one foot, then spin back toward the ball, pivoting on that same foot, and take a touch toward the starting cone with the inside of the opposite foot.
4. Cruyff turn: After running slightly past the ball, players use the inside of one foot to chop the ball behind the heel of the opposite foot, then use the outside of the opposite foot to take a touch and accelerate away.

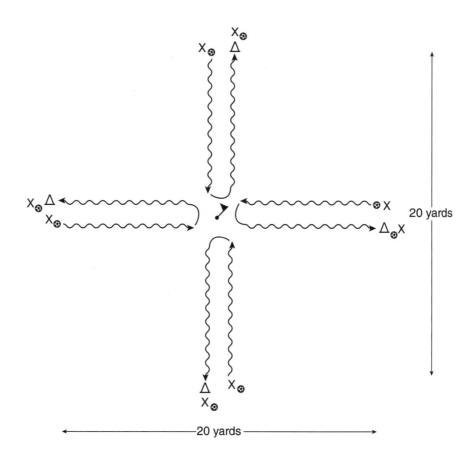

20 yards

20 yards

Purpose

Improve the ability to turn and dribble away from pressure by changing the dribbling angle, and improve overall ball control.

Organization

Place four cones 20 yards apart in the form of a cross, with one cone in the center (*a*). Two players stand in a line outside of each cone. Each player has a ball.

Procedure

The first player from each line dribbles to the center flag, changes the dribbling angle by stopping the ball with the sole of one foot, and pulls it back toward the body with the sole of that foot. The player then pushes the ball with the outside of the same foot toward the cone to the right.

Key Points

- Fake a shot before stopping the ball.
- The foot should not stop touching the ball between the stop, pull, and push.
- Perform using both feet.

Variations

1. Players lift the ball slightly with the outside of the foot when pushing it away.
2. Players stop, pull back, and push the ball toward the cone across the body with the inside of the foot.
3. Players spin away from, then move toward, the next cone using the inside of one foot (*b*).
4. Players spin away from, then move toward, the next cone using the outside of the foot.
5. Players use the outside-in step-over to get to the next cone.

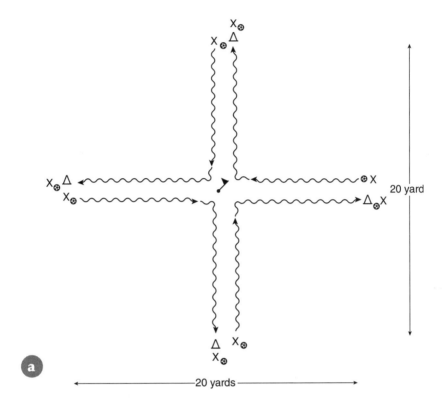

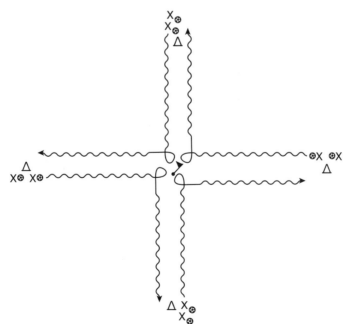

Purpose

Improve the ability to take on and get past an opponent, and improve overall ball control.

Organization

Place four cones 20 yards apart in the form of a cross. Create two lines of players at cones A and D. The line at cone A starts with the ball.

Procedure

Player 1 serves the ball across the diamond to player 2. Player 1 becomes the defender, and player 2 is the attacker. Player 2 tries to beat player 1 to any of the cones.

Cone A = 0 points

Cones B and C = 1 point

Cone D = 5 points

Defenders get one point for stealing or clearing the ball away.

Key Points

- Vary the speed in which you attack the defender.
- Dribble at an angle to create space for yourself.
- Change your pace after the defender is off balance.
- Retreat to cone A if you are unable to dribble past the defender, rather than concede possession.

Variations

1. Players play 2v1 to create more space, through passing, to dribble at the defenders. The attacking player can also use dribbling to get the defender to commit, thus freeing up the other attacking player for a pass.
2. Vary the type of service (weight, ground, bouncing, flighted) so that the attacking player has to control the ball quickly to dribble at the defender. This helps to create matchlike conditions, because players do not always receive the ball on the ground in a match.
3. Award 2 points for being able to pass to the next person at cone D.

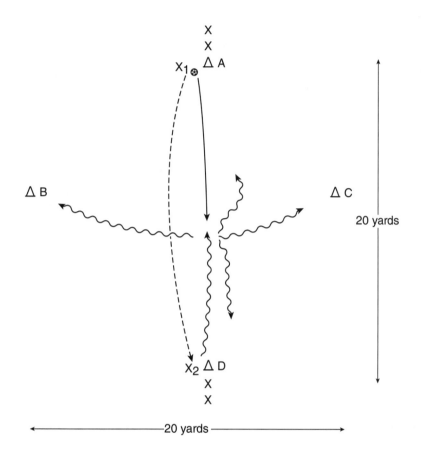

COMPETITIVE 1V1 DRIBBLING 2

Purpose

Improve the ability to take on and get past an opponent, and improve overall ball control.

Organization

Mark a 10- × 20-yard grid with cones or poles and place two small gates or goals at one end line.

Procedure

Player 1 serves the ball across the grid to player 2. Player 1 becomes the defender, and player 2 is the attacker. Player 2 tries to beat player 1 and dribble through either of the gates on the end line. The attacker gets 1 point for getting through the gates.

Key Points

- Vary the speed at which you attack the defender.
- Dribble at an angle to create space for yourself.
- Change your pace after the defender is off balance.
- Retreat when necessary to create space to run at the defender.

Variations

1. Attacking players use the entire end line, rather than two gates, to dribble across.
2. Using the gates, award a point for being able to pass the ball through either gate.
3. Set up additional gates on either sideline, close to one end line, and award points for being able to get through those gates.
4. Set up counter goals for the defender to attack if he steals the ball.
5. Players play 2v1 or 2v2 to create more variation and tactical situations, which creates more passing and dribbling options.

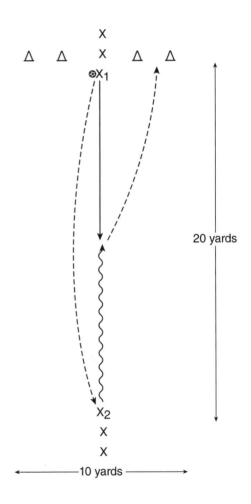

Purpose

Improve the ability to shield the ball from an opponent, and use open space to dribble away from pressure.

Organization

Mark a 20- × 30-yard grid (the size of the grid can vary based on the number of players). Players are in pairs, with one ball between them.

Procedure

On your signal, player 1 tries to retain possession of the ball while player 2 tries to steal it (like a game of Keep-Away). Players immediately switch roles if the ball is stolen or knocked out of bounds. Players play for 30-second bouts. The number of pairs is unlimited, and is based on the number of players training. After each bout, players should find a new partner. The number of total bouts should be between 5 and 10, with 30 seconds of rest between each bout.

Key Points

- Use your body to shield the ball.
- Keep the ball as far from defending as possible when shielding.
- Change your pace and dribble into open space to move away from pressure.

Variations

1. Players play one-minute bouts.
2. Make the grid larger to encourage dribbling into open space.
3. Make the grid smaller to force players to shield the ball more often.

27

COMPETITIVE DRIBBLING GAMES

Purpose

Improve overall dribbling ability.

Organization

Mark a 20- × 40-yard grid, including 5-yard-wide end zones running the length of each 40-yard sideline. (The grid size can vary based on the number of players.)

Procedure

Players play 4v4 (or higher with more players). Goals are scored by dribbling across the end line (*a*).

Key Points

- Choose the right moment to dribble to beat a player rather than dribbling to retain possession.
- Look for moments when there is a 1v1 matchup to dribble past an opponent.
- Change your pace to move past defenders.

Variations

1. Add one or two neutral, or plus, players to create more dribbling opportunities (*b*).
2. Use three or four small gates, as shown in *b*, rather than the entire end line for players to dribble through.

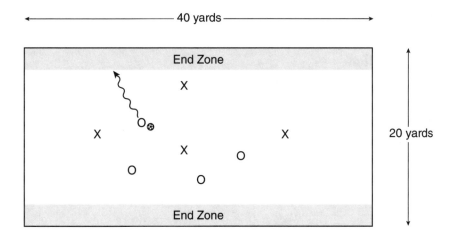

a

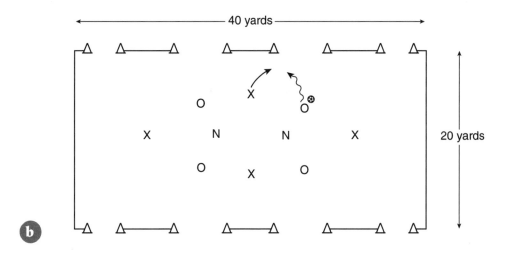

b

28

COMPETITIVE DRIBBLING GAMES: POSSESSION

Purpose
Improve overall dribbling ability.

Organization
Mark a 20- × 40-yard grid. (The grid size can vary based on the number of players.)

Procedure
Players play 4v4 (plus two neutral players). Players must take a minimum of three touches before passing to a teammate. A point is earned after seven passes.

Key Points
- Dribble into open space to move away from pressure.
- Shield the ball from a defender when necessary.
- Use fakes to create time on the ball and to open passing angles.

Variations
1. Make the grid larger to help players retain possession.
2. Increase or decrease the minimum number of touches.
3. Allow neutral players to play without touch restrictions.

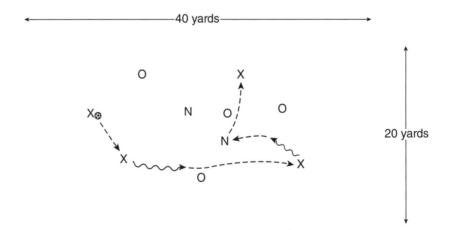

Purpose

Improve the ability to run at speed with the ball.

Organization

Mark a 44- × 60-yard field with regular goals. (The field size can vary based on the number of players.)

Procedure

Players play 7v7 (or lower or higher if necessary) to goal. Each player matches up with a player on the opposite team and can steal the ball only from that player. Players can steal the ball from anyone when it is being passed from player to player.

Key Points

- Have an attacking attitude. Look to dribble each time you have possession of the ball.
- Run with the ball at speed.
- Shield the ball from a defender when necessary.
- Use fakes to create time on the ball and to move past defenders.

Variations

1. Keep track of points between both individual pairs and the two teams.

2. Use teams of four, with each team matched up with another. This will encourage players to draw players toward them by dribbling and then use a pass when a player is free.

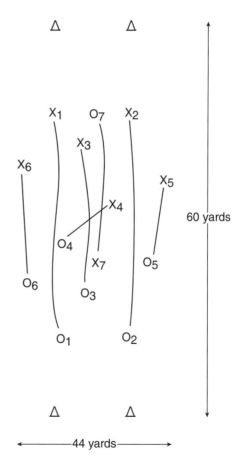

Purpose

Improve overall dribbling ability.

Organization

Create a 10- × 45-yard grid separated into nine 5-yard sections with cones or poles. One defender is in every other 5-yard section. Sections without defenders are neutral areas. Defenders cannot leave their sections.

Procedure

An attacker tries to dribble from one end of the grid to the other. If the attacker has the ball stolen, she takes the place of the defender who stole the ball, and the original defender joins the attacking line.

Key Points

- Unbalance the defender with a fake.
- Change your pace to move past the defender.
- Shield the ball from a defender when necessary.

Variations

1. Make the grid larger to help players retain possession.
2. Allow players to pass the ball into the next neutral zone to move past the defender.

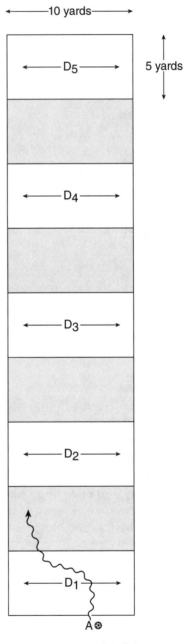

chapter 5

Passing and Receiving

The best teams in the world all have one thing in common: ball movement. At the club level, Barcelona, Real Madrid, Manchester United, Arsenal, Lyon, Ajax, and Bayern Munich circulate the ball quickly. At the international level, Brazil, Argentina, Italy, France, Spain, and Germany do as well. Those teams are the most fun to watch because of how they pass the ball around the field, and the rhythm their passing develops. Yes, they have great individual players, but how they play and pass the ball as a team is what makes them great.

Ball movement, at all levels, comes down to the ability to pass and receive the ball properly. If a player cannot control (receive) a pass from a teammate properly, or if a player cannot pass the ball properly, the entire game breaks down.

Being able to put the proper weight, pace, spin, and disguise on a pass, as well as getting the angle and accuracy of the pass correct, is essential for players who aspire to the highest levels, or those who simply aspire to the next level in their careers.

Along with the ability to play a pass properly, the ability to receive or control a pass correctly is crucial to a player's success.

Players must have many things, including speed, strength, and dribbling ability, to make it to the highest levels. However, the ability to function within a team at the top levels centers on a player's ability to perform the most basic elements: passing and receiving. At all levels of the game—youth, collegiate, professional, and international soccer—the best teams all are made up of players who are proficient in all forms of passing and receiving.

Why are passing and receiving so important? The simple answer is that they allow a team to retain possession of the ball during the game. With possession, a team creates scoring opportunities by quickly circulating the ball throughout the team, developing a rhythm, and moving the defending team out of position.

The more detailed answer to why passing and receiving are so important is that they provide players with time and space during a game. Many top coaches use the phrase *passing time on* to refer to effective passing. Essentially, the faster the ball moves to a teammate during passing, the more time that teammate will have on the ball before being closed down by a defender. With more time on the ball, players can make better decisions for their teams, because they do not have to deal with immediate pressure from the opposing team.

Players also can create more time for themselves by controlling the ball. If a player's first touch takes the ball exactly where she wants it to go, she has one fewer thing to worry about when deciding where to go next with the ball.

Finally, efficient passing and receiving allow players and teams to circulate the ball quickly around the field. The more quickly a team can move the ball, the more dangerous the team is when attacking.

The activities in this chapter will help players become more proficient when passing and receiving the ball. All are designed so that players must focus on the weight, pace, spin, angle, and accuracy of the pass, as well as receiving the ball with accuracy and from the best direction.

Purpose

Improve passing and receiving ability.

Organization

Create groups of 7 to 10 players. Players form a 20-yard circle, with two defenders in the center.

Procedure

Outside players stay connected by holding a bib between each player. Playing two-touch, outside players try to keep the ball away from the two defending players. When defending players touch or steal the ball, the player who turned the ball over replaces the defending player who has been in the longest. If outside players connect 10 or more passes in a row or split the two defending players with a pass, the two defending players stay for another round.

Key Points

- Take the first touch away from pressure.
- Zip the ball across when passing (pass time on).
- Make the time between the control and the pass as short as possible.

Variations

1. Players play one-touch.
2. Outside players do not hold bibs.

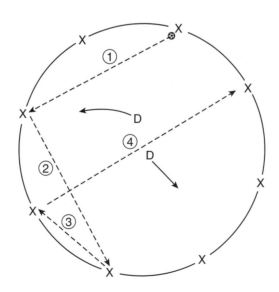

Purpose

Improve short passing and receiving ability.

Organization

Create two groups of four to eight players. Players form two lines 10 to 15 yards apart.

Procedure

Player 1 passes the ball across to player 2 and follows the pass. In two touches, player 2 controls and passes the ball across to player 3, follows the pass, and so on (a).

Key Points

- Zip the ball across when passing (pass time on).
- Take a good first touch to prepare the ball for the pass.
- Make the time between the control and the pass as short as possible.

Variations

1. Players take only one touch at each end.
2. Players double-pass at each end.
3. After receiving, players dribble halfway across and then pass while on the run.
4. Increase the distance so that the passes are flighted and players must receive balls out of the air.
5. Player 2 checks to center to receive the ball from player 1. After receiving the ball, player 2 turns away from player 1, who has followed his pass. Player 2 passes the ball into the path of player 1, focusing on the proper weight of the pass. Player 1 then passes to player 4 in one touch. Players repeat from the opposite side (b).
6. Player 1 starts by dribbling the ball at an angle. He then passes the ball to player 2 and follows his pass to perform a double pass, or one-two, with player 2. Player 2 repeats with player 3.
7. Add a second ball. Players 1 and 2 pass across at the same time.
    a. Players pass across, dribble, and switch balls in the center.
    b. Players pass across, dribble, switch balls once, then switch balls twice.

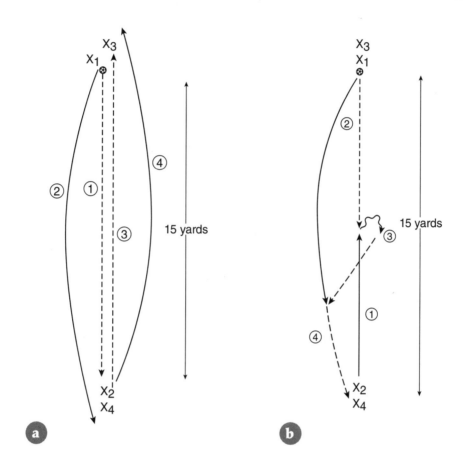

33

GROUPS OF FOUR

Purpose

Improve passing and receiving ability.

Organization

Create groups of four as shown; use two balls.

Procedure

Players 1 and 2 pass to players 3 and 4 at the same time. Players 3 and 4 receive and pass back to players 1 and 2, then turn to receive from the opposite side *(a)*.

Key Points

- Zip the ball across when passing (pass time on).
- Take a good first touch to prepare the ball for a pass.
- Make the time between the control and the pass as short as possible.
- Keep your feet moving before receiving the ball.

Variations

1. Players take only one touch.
2. Players 3 and 4 start with the ball and double-pass at each end.
3. After receiving the ball, players 3 and 4 turn and pass to the opposite side, then turn back to get the next ball from their original partners *(b)*.
4. Increase the distance so that the passes are flighted and players must receive balls out of the air.
5. Players 1 and 2 must juggle the ball and play to players 3 and 4 in the air.

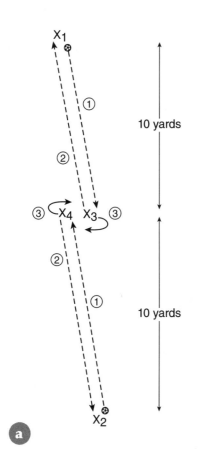

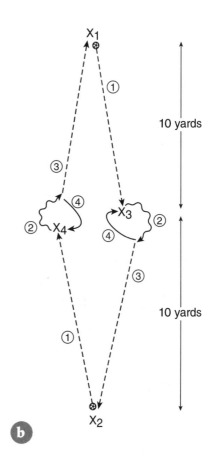

10 yards

10 yards

10 yards

10 yards

34

TRIANGLE PASSING

Purpose

Improve passing and receiving ability.

Organization

Create groups of four to eight players. Players form a triangle, 15 to 20 yards on each side.

Procedure

Player 1 passes the ball across to player 2 and follows the pass, moving to the end of player 2's line. In two touches, player 2 controls and passes the ball across to player 3, who does the same, passing to player 4 (a).

Key Points

- Take the first touch across the body when receiving.
- Zip the ball across when passing (pass time on).
- Take a good first touch to prepare the ball for a pass.
- Make the time between the control and the pass as short as possible.

Variations

1. After receiving, players dribble halfway across and then pass while on the run.
2. Players double-pass at each end: Player 1 passes to player 2, and in quick succession, player 2 passes to player 1, and player 1 passes back to player 2 (b).
3. Add a second ball. Players 1 and 2 both start with a ball and begin the activity by passing to players 3 and 4 simultaneously.
4. Increase the distance so that the players must hit the ball along the ground with more pace.

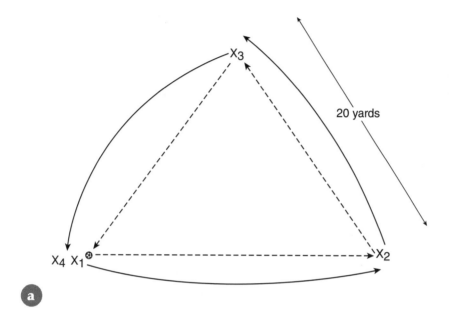

a

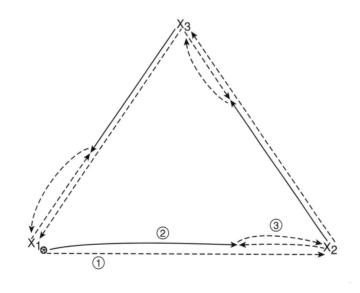

b

35

RECTANGLE PASSING

Purpose

Improve passing and receiving ability.

Organization

Create groups of 6 to 10 players. Players form a rectangle, 15 × 40 yards.

Procedure

Player 1 plays a short pass to player 2. In two touches, player 2 controls and plays a long, flighted pass to player 3, who controls and plays a short pass to player 4. Player 4 controls and plays a long pass to player 5, continuing on in a short, long, short sequence until all players have had a play (a).

Key Points

- Overhit the long pass.
- Take a good first touch to prepare the ball for a pass.
- Make the time between the control and the pass as short as possible.

Variations

1. Players double-pass after each long pass.
2. Players take only one touch.
3. Player 1 plays a long ball to player 2, who lays the ball off for player 1. Player 1 passes to player 3, who plays a long ball to player 4, who lays the ball off for player 3. Player 3 passes to player 5, who repeats the sequence (b).
4. Add a second or third ball.

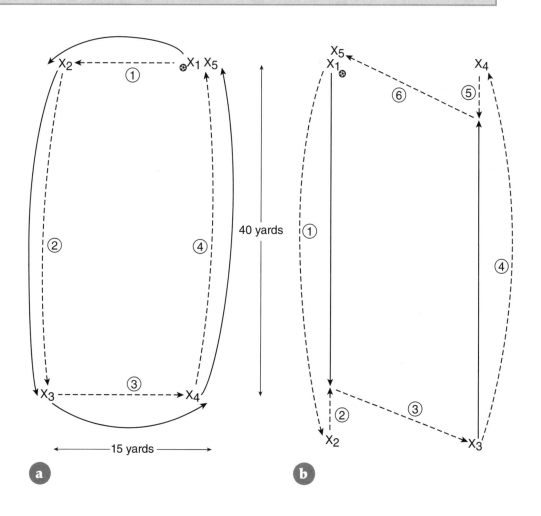

Purpose

Improve passing and receiving ability.

Organization

Give two balls to two groups of 7 to 12 players. Place outside cones 10 yards from the center cone.

Procedure

At the same time, players 1 and 5 pass balls to players 2 and 6. In two touches, players 2 and 6 control and pass to players 3 and 7, who do the same, passing to players 4 and 8 *(a)*.

Key Points

- Take the first touch across the body when receiving.
- Zip the ball across when passing (pass time on).
- Take a good first touch to prepare the ball for a pass.
- Make the time between the control and the pass as short as possible.

Variations

1. Players play a one-two at points A and B. A one-two is a give-and-go, or a back-and-forth pass *(b)*.
2. Players dribble the ball halfway across, then pass.
3. Reverse the direction, or rotation, of the passes.
4. Increase the distance so that the players must hit the ball along the ground with more pace.

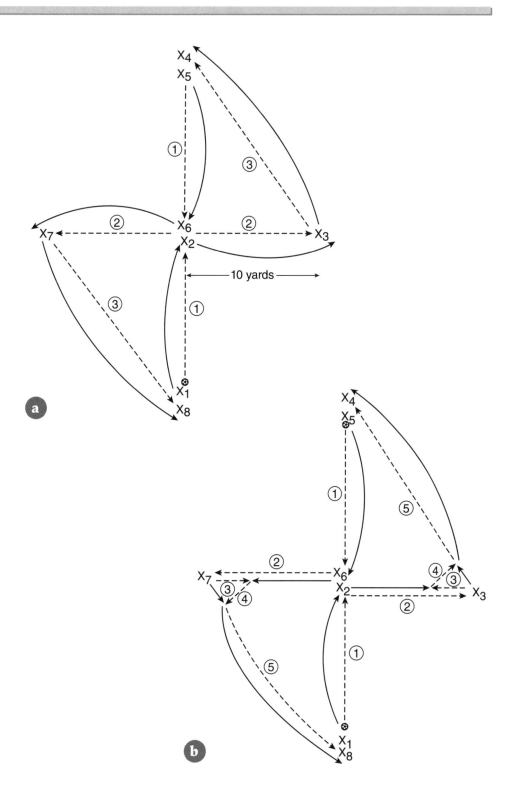

4V2 (+2)

Purpose

Improve passing and receiving ability.

Organization

In a 20- × 60-yard grid, create two teams of four players. The coach stands at the midway point of the sideline with balls at his feet (a).

Procedure

Start play by serving a ball into one side of the grid. The team in possession attempts to connect 4 to 8 passes and play the ball back across the middle for a point. The defending team sends two players to defend the four, attempting to either knock the ball out of bounds or steal the ball and play it back across the middle to their teammates. A point is scored for the defending team only when they steal and play back across successfully. Players play three-minute rounds.

Key Points

- Take a positive first touch into space and away from pressure.
- Pass time on when playing to a teammate.
- To avoid having the ball stolen, make the time between the control and the pass as short as possible (b).

Variation

Add touch restrictions:

1. Two touches
2. One touch
3. Three touches

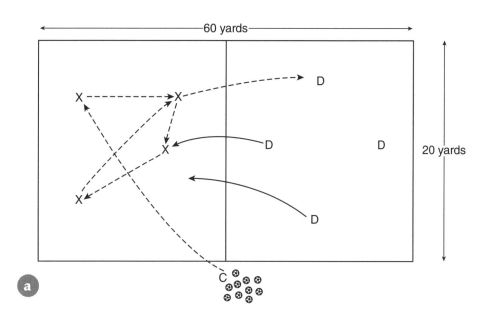

Purpose

Improve passing and receiving ability.

Organization

Separate groups of 16 into 8 pairs. Half the pairs go to the center of a circle formed by the remaining eight players, who have a ball each. The diameter of the circle should be between 30 and 40 yards.

Procedure

Players 1 and 2 check to player 3. Player 3 passes the ball to player 1, who controls, passes back to player 3, and spins out. Player 3 passes to player 2, who controls, passes back, and follows player 1 to the next pass. All four pairs in the center are moving at the same time. Players play for one minute, then rotate positions.

Key Points

- Zip the ball across when passing (pass time on).
- Take a good first touch to prepare the ball for a pass.
- Make the time between the control and the pass as short as possible.

Variations

1. Player 1 dummies the ball between his legs for player 2, who controls and passes back to player 3. A dummy is when a player lets a ball that is passed to her roll between her legs or past her for another player to receive.

2. Player 1 controls, passes back to player 3, then "bumps off" to play a one-two with player 2. *Bumping off* means that the player who has just passed moves backward a few yards to create open space for the return pass.

3. Player 3 throws the ball to players 1 and 2, who perform volleys, or control the ball to the ground and then pass it back.

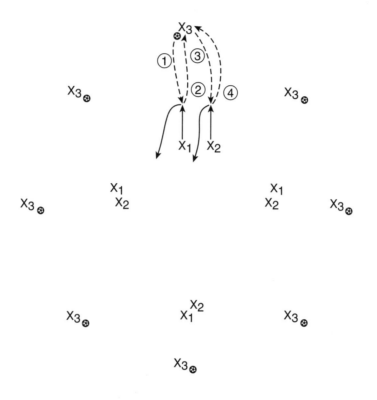

PAIRS

Purpose

Improve passing and receiving ability.

Organization

Separate groups of four players into two pairs on opposite sides of a 40-yard area.

Procedure

Player 1 serves the ball to player 3, and then switches spots with player 2. Player 3 receives the ball, lays it off for player 4, and bumps backward to make space for a return pass. Player 4 plays the ball back to player 3, who serves across to player 2.

Key Points

- Overhit long passes.
- Get in line with the ball when receiving.
- Bump off to create enough room for a pass and serve.

Variations

1. Player 1 plays the ball across on the ground. Player 3 dummies the ball between his legs for player 4. Player 4 plays a one-two with player 3 and then serves the ball back across for player 1 to dummy.
2. Shorten the distance for shorter, ground passing.

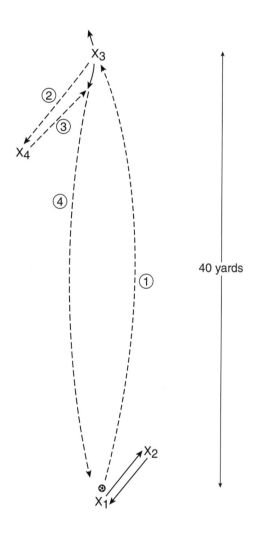

40 yards

Purpose
Improve passing and receiving ability.

Organization
Players 1 and 2 stand, each with a ball, at either end of a 10- to 20-yard area. Player 3 stands in the middle, equidistant to players 1 and 2.

Procedure
Player 1 serves the ball to player 3, who checks back to player 1 to receive the pass. Player 3 then plays the ball back to player 1, and then spins out to check for a new pass from player 2. Player 2 passes to player 3, who receives, passes back, and checks back to player 1. Players repeat for one minute (a).

Key Points
- Take the first touch to the outside of the body.
- Fake before receiving the ball.
- Weight pass properly.
- Make the time between the control and the pass as short as possible.

Variations
1. Players 1 and 2 throw balls to player 3. Player 3 performs any of the following:
   a. Inside-of-the-foot volley
   b. Laces volley
   c. Header
   d. Chest, then volley
   e. Chest, control to ground, pass
2. Players 1 and 2 juggle the ball and serve out of the air, rather than holding the ball.
3. Players use one ball. Player 3 checks to player 1, receives the pass, and turns, immediately passing to player 2. After player 2 has received the pass, player 1 checks to player 2, receives the pass, and turns, playing a pass back to player 1.
4. Players use one ball. Player 1 passes to player 2 and follows the pass, rounding player 2 to receive a short pass on the opposite side. Player 1 then plays a long pass to player 3 and follows the pass, rounding player 3 to receive to receive a short pass on the opposite side. Player 1 finishes by dribbling back to the starting point (b).

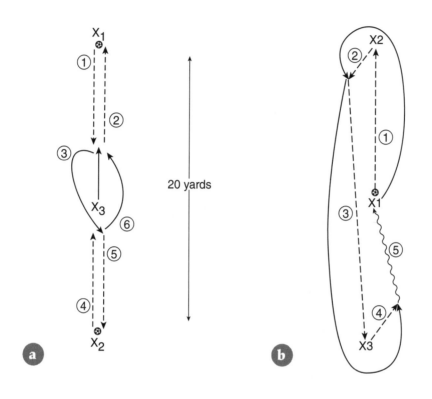

WINDOWS

Purpose

Improve passing and receiving ability.

Organization

Use eight balls for 16 players. Eight players form a large circle, each with a ball at his or her feet. The diameter of the circle should be 30 to 40 yards. The remaining eight players stand in the center of the circle.

Procedure

At your signal, each of the eight inside players checks back to one of the outside players to receive a pass. In two touches, each inside player controls and returns the pass to an outside player, then turns and finds another outside player to receive a pass from. Players repeat for two minutes (a).

Key Points

- Vary the controlling surface when receiving.
- Vary the passing surface when passing.
- Fake before receiving the ball.
- Weight pass properly.
- Make the time between the control and the pass as short as possible.

Variations

1. Inside players receive the ball and turn, dribble, then pass to any outside player.
2. Inside players start with the ball, pass to an outside player, follow the pass, and overlap the outside player. The outside player passes the ball back into the path of the inside player (b).
3. Outside players throw the ball as the inside players check back. Inside players perform any of the following:
   a. Headers
   b. Inside-of-the-foot volley
   c. Laces volley
   d. Chest, then volley
   e. Chest, thigh, volley

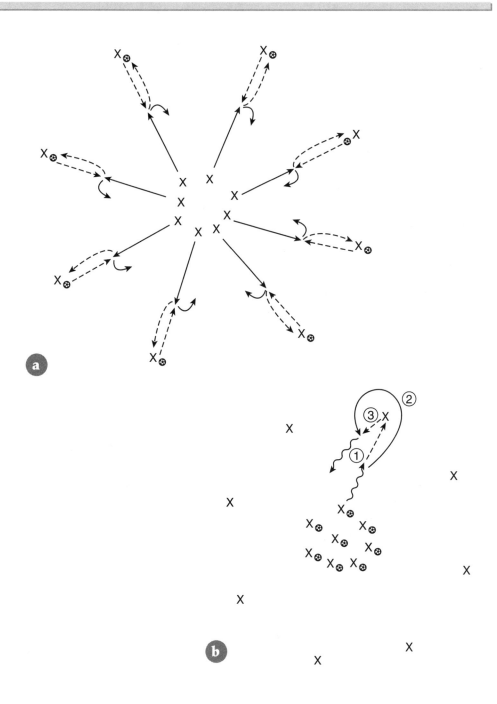

Purpose

Improve passing and receiving ability.

Organization

Give two balls to each group of seven players. Players organize themselves as shown. Balls start with players 1 and 2. The ball is passed in a zigzag sequence from one end of the line to the other.

Procedure

At your signal, player 1 plays a pass to player 3, and follows the pass to take player 3's spot. Player 3 controls the ball, passes to player 4, and takes player 4's spot. Player 4 controls the ball, passes to player 5, and takes player 5's spot. Player 5 passes to player 6 and goes to the end of player 6's line. Player 6 dribbles the ball across to continue the sequence (a).

When the first ball reaches player 4, player 2 starts the second ball, performing the same sequence, so that two balls are in play at the same time.

Key Points

- Receive the pass across the body.
- Fake before receiving the ball.
- Zip the pass across to the next player.
- Make the time between the control and the pass as short as possible.

Variations

1. Players 1 and 3, 3 and 4, and 4 and 5 perform a one-two when exchanging the ball.
2. Player 1 passes to player 3. Player 3 lays the ball back to player 1, who passes to player 4. Player 4 lays the ball back to player 3, who passes to player 5, and so on (b).
3. Player 6 controls the pass and then plays a long, flighted pass back to the beginning, rather than dribbling across.

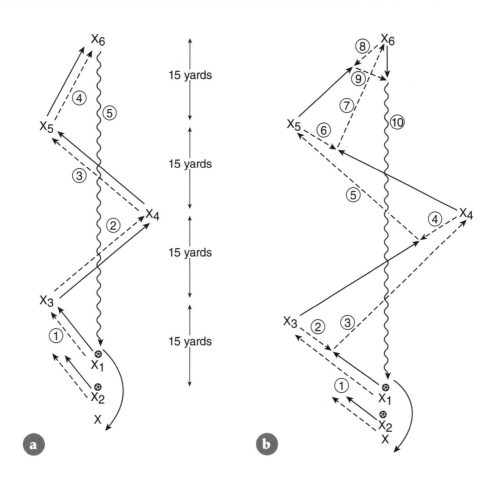

Purpose

Improve passing and receiving ability.

Organization

Players stand in two rows with one ball per two players. Player 1 starts with the ball. Player 2 faces player 1, standing 3 yards away.

Procedure

At your signal, player 1 passes to player 2 and moves forward. Player 2 passes the ball back to player 1 and jogs backward. The pairs repeat the sequence across a 40- to 60-yard area. Once the players reach the sideline, they repeat the sequence back across, with player 2 passing and moving forward and player 1 jogging backward.

Key Points

- Stay balanced.
- Vary the surface of the foot for passing and receiving.
- Weight pass properly.
- Make the time between the control and the pass as short as possible.

Variations

1. Allow only one touch per player.
2. Headers: Players must keep the ball in the air for each pass with a header and a volley return.
3. Volleys
   a. All passes must be made with the inside of the foot.
   b. All passes must be made from the laces.
   c. Side volleys: The serving player throws the ball slightly to the side of the receiving player.
4. Players must control with the chest before volleying it back to player 2.

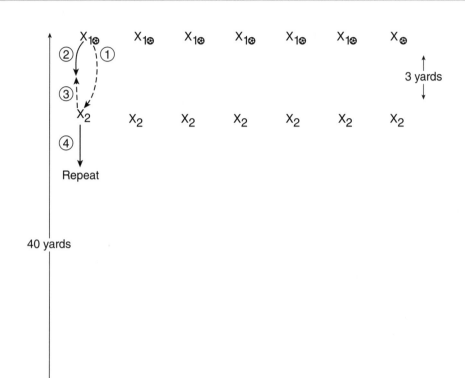

Purpose

Improve passing and receiving ability.

Organization

Organize groups of six players. Players 3 and 4 stay in the center for two minutes, then rotate with two other players.

Procedure

At your signal, player 1 passes across to player 2 and overlaps player 2. Player 2 controls and passes to player 3, who has checked back for the ball. Player 3 lays the ball back to player 1, who passes to player 4. Player 4 lays the ball back for player 2, who controls and passes to player 5. The players repeat the sequence going back across. Players repeat for two to four minutes (*a*).

Key Points

- Control the ball in the direction you will be passing.
- Time runs properly.
- Weight pass properly.
- Make the time between the control and the pass as short as possible.

Variations

1. Player 3 dummies the ball for player 4 and spins to face player 4. Player 4 lays the ball off to player 3, who passes into the path of player 1. Player 1 passes across to player 2. Player 2 passes to player 5, who starts the sequence in the opposite direction (*b*).
2. Increase distances for longer passing.
3. Require players to play with one touch.

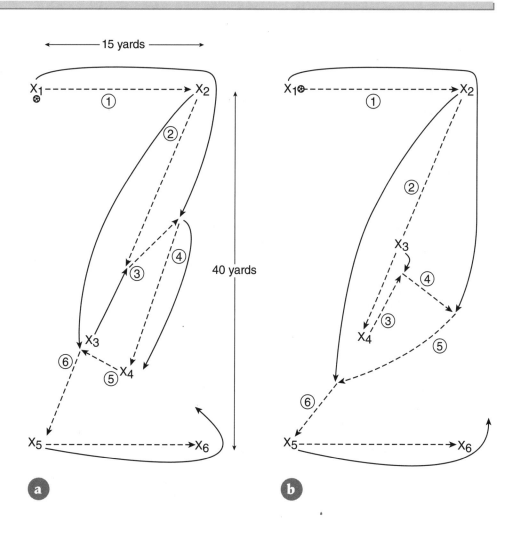

Purpose

Improve passing and receiving ability.

Organization

Create groups of 12 to 16 players. Eight to twelve players form a large circle (30 to 40 yards in diameter), depending on the total number of available players. The four remaining players, each with a ball, stand inside the circle.

Procedure

Player 1 dribbles toward, then passes to, player 2 and takes player 2's spot. Player 2 passes to player 3 and takes player 3's spot. Player 3 dribbles into the circle, passes to player 4, and takes player 4's spot. Player 4 passes to player 5 and takes player 5's spot. Player 5 dribbles into the circle, and the sequence repeats. Four balls are in play at the same time. Players repeat for three minutes.

Key Points

- Weight pass properly.
- Make the time between the control and the pass as short as possible.

Variations

1. Player 1 passes to player 2 and follows the pass. Player 2 passes back to player 1. Player 1 passes to player 3 and takes player 3's spot. Player 3 dribbles into the circle and repeats the sequence.

2. Player 1 passes to player 2. Player 2 passes to player 3 and overlaps player 3. Player 3 passes to player 1, who passes to player 2 and then takes player 1's spot. Player 1 dribbles into the circle and repeats the sequence.

3. Player 1 passes to player 2 and follows the pass. Players 2 and 3 perform a one-two around player 1. Player 2 ends with the ball and dribbles inside the circle to repeat the sequence.

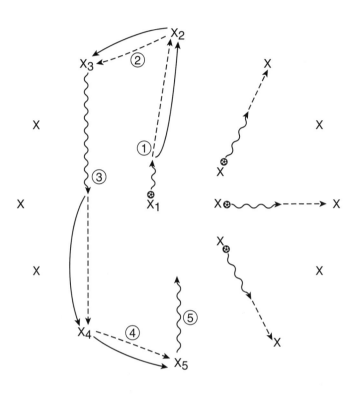

chapter 6

Heading

Over the past 20 years, the United States and its players have made great strides in professional soccer. The U.S. national team has qualified for the previous five World Cups, made a quarterfinal appearance in 2002, and held a number 4 FIFA world ranking in April 2005. American players are now playing in some of the best leagues in the world. Brian McBride, who currently plays for and is the captain of Fulham FC in England's Premier League, is regarded as America's best header of the ball. However, most top-level coaches will agree that, particularly at the youth level, the one skill that American players are not competent at is heading the ball. At all levels of the game in the United States, our players lose opportunities because of a lack of heading quality. Whether they miss a headed scoring chance or passing chance, or simply concede territory, American players' lack of quality heading has a negative impact on their chances for success in most games.

Other international players who are known for their ability to head the ball are England and Chelsea's John Terry, Liverpool's Peter Crouch, and Germany and Bayern Munich's Miroslav Klose. All three have the ability to change a game based on their ability to head the ball effectively.

The most famous example of heading ability having a significant impact on a game was in the 1998 World Cup Final between France and Brazil. That game was largely decided by two headed goals, from corner kicks, by Zinedine Zidane.

A large part of the problem in the United States is that not enough heading is done in training. Functional repetition, particularly with heading, is necessary in order for players to be comfortable and excel at heading the ball. It is crucial that coaches put players in positions to practice all three types of heading. Consider how defenders on teams in the English Premier League practice. The coach places the two central defenders deep in their own half of the field and then splays long, flighted balls to them so they can practice the techniques and timing used to perform a clearing header. Many teams also do the same exercise as part of warm-ups prior to matches. In addition, many of the best forwards spend time after training each day practicing heading crosses into the goal.

Attacking Heading

Generally, in the penalty box or in the attacking third, attacking heading is done to try to score a goal from a cross or flighted ball. When heading the ball in an attacking manner, and on goal, players generally head the ball down, toward the feet of the goalkeeper. The body mechanics can vary slightly, but oftentimes the attacking player jumps, attempts to make contact with the top of the ball, and snaps his head and upper body in the direction he wants the ball to go. The snap action is what generates not only the direction, but more importantly, the power of the header. Players must also try to keep their eyes on the ball throughout the header.

For a successful attacking header, the head and upper body should snap in the direction the player wishes the ball to go.

Head Passing

Head passing is more subtle than attacking or defending heading. It often requires the ability to redirect the ball to a teammate, or to open space, and the ability to increase or decrease the speed of the ball.

Using a header to pass the ball can obviously be done in any area of the field. For this reason, all players should be adept at head passing. Unlike attacking headers, in which the snap action generates power, head passing requires a player to use her head and upper body to set, or guide, the ball to a teammate. With head passing, power is not the goal; rather, the goal is accuracy and weighting the pass properly so that a teammate can control and use the ball as quickly and easily as possible.

The flick header, in which a player skims, or flicks, the ball backward, is also a very important form of head passing. The player skims the bottom of the ball with the top of the head to gain territory or pass to a teammate. As the ball makes contact with the head, the player flicks, or snaps, the head backward. A center forward often uses this move to flick a long, aerial ball backward for another forward to run to. The flick header can also be used to gain territory from a throw-in. The player throws the ball down the line to a teammate's head; that teammate then flicks the ball backward into space or to another teammate.

Defensive Heading

Defensive heading is primarily done in the defending third of the field to clear the ball from danger. Because the general goal is to clear the ball, players should attempt to get as much height and distance on the ball as possible. Players should bend their knees slightly prior to making contact and then spring, or explode, through the bottom of the ball to generate the necessary height and distance.

The following activities cover all three types of headers in a variety of ways. They are designed so that players can maximize repetitions in functional, gamelike situations.

HEAD PASSING

Purpose

Improve head passing.

Organization

Form groups of three players, each with one ball. Player 1 stands 20 yards from players 2 and 3.

Procedure

Player 1 punts the ball toward player 2. As the ball travels, player 3 positions himself underneath player 2, ready to receive a head pass. Player 2 positions himself and performs a head pass to player 3. Players 2 and 3 then reverse roles for player 1's next punt *(a)*.

Key Points

- Set, or guide, the ball when head passing.
- Use peripheral vision to locate the player receiving the pass.

Variation

Flick header: Player 1 punts to player 2. While the ball is traveling, player 3 pulls wide and then runs in behind player 2, who flicks the punt for player 3 to run to *(b)*.

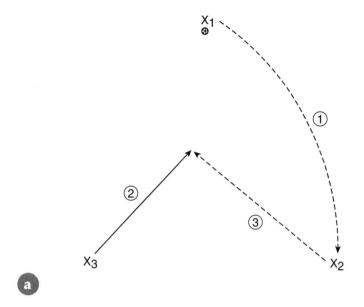

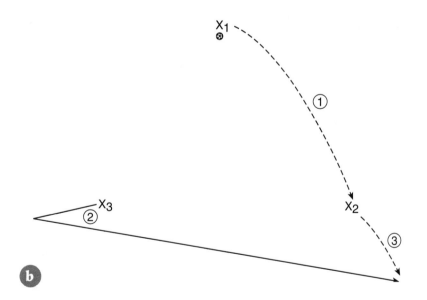

Purpose

Improve overall heading ability.

Organization

Form groups of three players, each with one ball. In a 10-yard line, player 2 stands between players 1 and 3. Player 1 starts with the ball.

Procedure

Player 1 throws or serves the ball to player 2. Player 2 head passes back to player 1, who heads the ball over player 2 to player 3. Player 3 head passes to player 2. Player 2 head passes back to player 3, who heads the ball back over player 2 to player 1. Players repeat back and forth for two minutes, then rotate the player in the middle *(a)*.

Key Points

- Make contact with the appropriate part of the ball.
- When heading over the middle player, bend the knees and spring through the bottom of the ball.
- Set, or guide, the ball when head passing.

Variation

Flick header: Player 1 serves the ball for player 2 to flick to player 3. Player 3 head passes back to player 2, who flicks the ball back to player 1. Players repeat back and forth for two minutes and then rotate *(b)*.

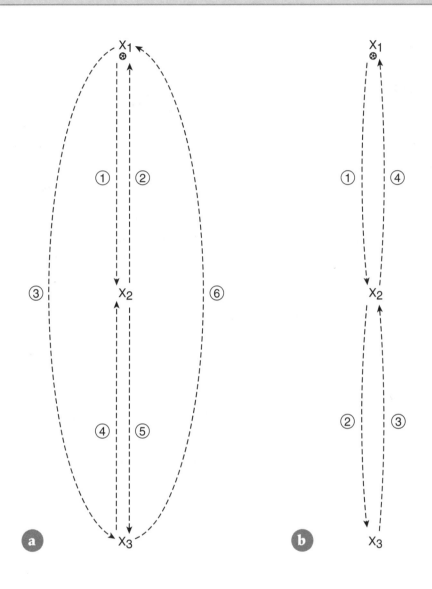

Purpose

Improve attacking heading.

Organization

Form groups of four players, each with one ball. Players 1 and 2 are partners, and players 3 and 4 are partners. Each set of partners defends a goal. The playing area is 20 × 10 yards, with a goal, marked with poles or cones, in the center.

Procedure

Players 1 and 2 head juggle toward the goal that players 3 and 4 are defending. At any point, player 1 or player 2 can attempt to score a goal, with a header, on players 3 and 4. After players 1 and 2 have attempted to score, players 3 and 4 do the same, moving toward the goal that players 1 and 2 are defending. Players go back and forth for two minutes or until one pair reaches five goals; then they switch partners (a).

Key Points

- Head the ball down when attempting to score.
- Jump and snap the head and upper body in the direction of the goal.
- If the ball hits the ground while head juggling, it is a turnover.
- You can use any part of your body to keep the ball in the air, but you must use your head to score.
- The defending pair acts as goalkeepers and can use their hands.

Variation

Players head juggle forward and back, rather than side to side, so that player 2 stands with her back to the goal and sets the ball for player 1 to head on goal (b).

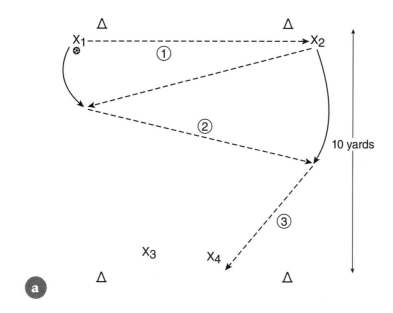

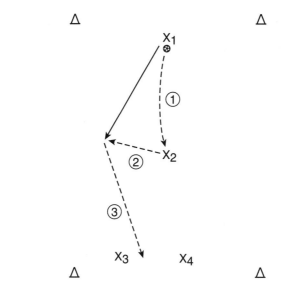

FLICK HEADERS

Purpose

Improve overall heading ability.

Organization

Form groups of four players, each with one ball. In a 15-yard line, players 2 and 3 stand between players 1 and 4. Player 1 starts with the ball.

Procedure

Player 1 throws or serves the ball to player 2, who flicks it backward to player 3. Player 3 flicks the ball backward to player 4, who head passes it back to player 3. Player 3 flicks to player 2, who flicks to player 1. Players repeat back and forth for two minutes, and then rotate the middle players (a).

Key Points

- Make contact with the appropriate part of the ball.
- Set, or guide, the ball when head passing.

Variations

1. Player 1 throws or serves to player 2, who flicks to player 3. Player 3 head passes back to player 2, who head passes back to player 3. Player 3 flicks to player 4, who then passes back to player 3. Players repeat back and forth for two minutes, and then rotate the middle players.

2. Player 1 throws or serves to player 2, who head passes back to player 1. Player 1 head passes over player 2 to player 3, who head passes to player 2. Player 2 head passes over player 3 to player 4. Players repeat back and forth for two minutes, and then rotate the middle players (b).

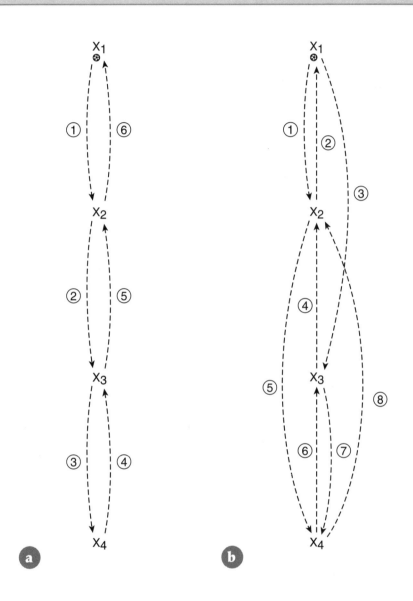

Purpose

Improve attacking heading ability.

Organization

Form two teams, A and B, from a group of 10 to 18 players, each with 10 balls. Teams A and B stand in two lines at the top of the penalty box on either side of the arc, or D. Servers A and B stand, with five balls each, between the edge of the box and the corner of the field.

Procedure

Server A serves a flighted ball into the penalty box. Player A1 runs into the box and heads the ball on goal, attempting to score. As soon as player A1 has attempted to score, server B serves a flighted ball for player B1 to head on goal. Players repeat back and forth for five minutes, keeping score, or until one team has scored five goals; then they rotate so that players on each team get a chance to be a server *(a)*.

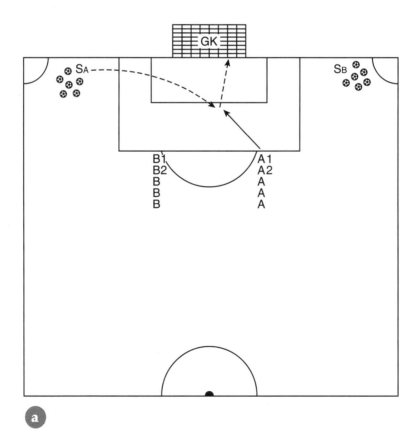

Key Points

- Make contact with the middle or top of the ball.
- Snap the head and upper body to generate power.
- Head the ball down at the goalkeeper's feet.

Variations

1. Players A1 and A2 run into the box, one to the near post and one to the far post, and attempt to finish the cross from the server.

2. Players B1 and B2 run into the box, one to the near post and one to the far post. Server B serves the ball to the near post, where player B1 flicks the ball to player B2 to finish with the head or feet *(b)*.

3. 1v1: Server A serves and player A1 attempts to score; player B1 must defend and clear the served ball.

4. Server A serves a deep cross. Player A1 head passes down to player A2's feet. Player A2 shoots or finishes on goal, with the feet.

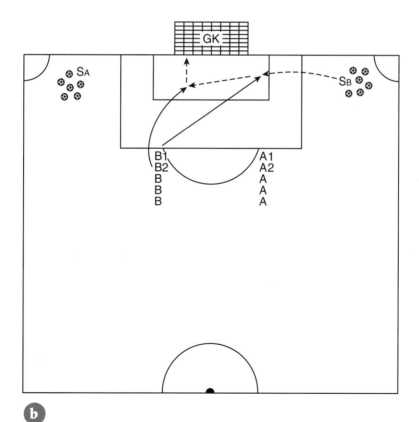

b

51   COMPETITIVE HEADERS ON GOAL

Purpose

Improve attacking and defending heading ability.

Organization

Form two teams, A and B, from a group of 10 to 18 players, each with 10 balls. Teams A and B stand in the penalty box. Team A is attacking the goal; team B is defending the goal. Servers 1, 2, 3, and 4 position themselves, with balls, at each corner of the penalty box (*a*).

Procedure

Call out a number from 1 to 4. The corresponding server serves a ball into the box for teams A and B to compete for. Team A attempts to score, and team B attempts to clear. The ball is live until scored, cleared, or hit out of bounds. Players repeat for three minutes and then rotate servers and teams in the box.

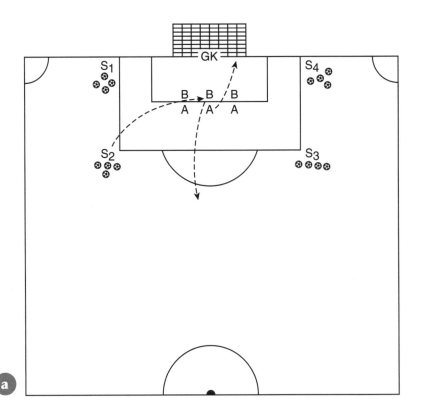

Key Points

- Attacking: Head the ball down. Position for a head pass, flick, rebound, or knockdown.

- Defending: Clear with height and distance. Spring through the bottom of the ball. Be alert for flicks and knockdowns.

Variations

1. Position servers 2 and 3 farther from the goal so that their crosses are from different angles *(b)*.

2. Add server 5, in the center of the field, 10 yards inside the halfway line.

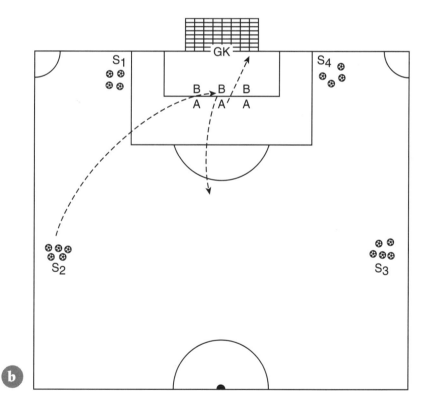

52 HANDBALL WITH HEADERS TO SCORE

Purpose
Improve overall heading ability.

Organization
Form groups of 10 to 18 players, each with one ball. In one half of the field, teams A and B each attack a goal (see diagram).

Procedure
Players pass the ball by throwing and catching. They may run with the ball until tagged, but then must stand still and pass. To score, the team must head the ball into the goal.

Key Points
- Head the ball down when attempting to score.
- If the ball is dropped, it is a turnover.
- Players cannot knock the ball out of an opposing player's hands.

Variation
Players play the same game but must pass the ball using a throw-head-catch pattern.

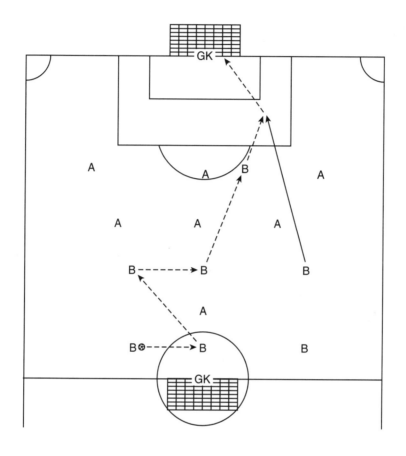

CLEARING HEADERS

Purpose

Improve defensive heading.

Organization

Form groups of three players, each with one ball. Player 1 stands 20 yards from players 2 and 3.

Procedure

Player 1 punts the ball toward player 2. As the ball travels, player 2 positions himself to perform a clearing header over player 1, while player 3 drops off to cover behind player 2. On the next punt, players 2 and 3 then reverse roles for player 1's next serve.

Key Points

- Bend your knees prior to contact and spring through the ball.
- Make contact with the bottom of the ball.
- Keep your eyes open and mouth closed.

Variations

1. Competitive headers: Player 1 punts the ball toward players 2 and 3, who compete, 1v1, to head the ball back to player 1.
2. Player 3 stands directly behind player 2. Player 1 serves or throws the ball so that player 3 has to jump over player 2's back to make contact with the ball.

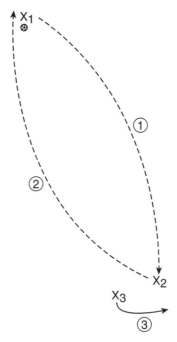

chapter 7

Attacking and Defending

To develop players, as well as teams, you must have training activities and exercises that replicate a match environment as closely as possible. Lt. Col. H.T. Hayden, a successful U.S. marine, wrote the following in his 1995 book titled *Warfighting*.

> Exercises should approximate the conditions of battle as much as possible; that is, they should introduce friction in the form of uncertainty, stress, disorder, and opposing wills. This last characteristic is most important; only in opposed, free play exercises can we practice the art of war. Dictated or "canned" scenarios eliminate the element of independent, opposing wills that is the essence of combat.

Clearly, soccer is not war. However, there are similarities between the two in terms of training for success. Training activities for the game of soccer are most effective when they replicate the randomness and competitive nature of matches.

The most critical component in soccer is transition, from attack to defense, and from defense to attack. At the highest levels, the ability of players and teams to transition quickly is the difference between winning and losing. The only way to train players to make successful transitions is to replicate the conditions of a match. You can do this by using a variety of games, conditions, and field spaces during practices.

By nature, the elite player is extremely competitive and wants to win in every situation. Simply having a winner and a loser creates a match environment in practice. You can also create a competitive atmosphere by counting points, passes, and goals, or by simply setting a time limit.

Making the field space larger or smaller during training changes the demands of the game. When the field space is smaller, players have less time to control the ball and make decisions when in possession. With a larger field space, players have more time on the ball, yet must transition faster on both sides of the ball to exploit the increased space.

Placing touch restrictions on players during training games forces them to think and play more quickly, similar to the way they will have to think and play during a match. When they are limited to one or two touches on the ball, the players have to adjust their bodies to play more quickly, think in advance of the current play, and control the ball cleanly.

The use of neutral zones in training games won't necessarily put more restrictive pressure on players, but using them will allow players to work on a specific area of attack. For example, when there are "free" wide spaces, players are encouraged to play the ball to the wide player in the free zone, highlighting the wide attacking play. Using neutral zones helps players develop patterns and recognize the cues of the game, and it instills a general playing style within a team.

Using multiple goals in training exercise can serve a variety of functions. The most obvious is creating more scoring situations. When multiple goals are used, the field space is usually wider than it is long. This encourages attacking players to move the ball from side to side, develop rhythm, and attempt to stretch the defending team to create scoring opportunities.

Practicing slide tackles within a narrowed field space highlights the approach and the importance of making contact with the ball (instead of the opponent), which helps players learn to make quick and successful transitions from defense to attack.

On the other side of the ball, the defending team must focus sharply on staying connected, moving as a group, and recognizing when to press the ball and when to drop off.

Often, coaches use neutral, or plus, players in training. A neutral player plays for whichever team has the ball and then changes to the opposite team when possession is lost. The numerical advantage that neutral players give to the team in possession results in the defending team having to concentrate and transition quickly to win the ball back. Staying compact and moving as a group is crucial for defenders because the opposite team has a numerical advantage. The team in possession, meanwhile, must use its numerical advantage; quickly expanding the playing field by spacing out the attacking players, for example, makes defending difficult.

Purpose

Improve attacking and defending shape, positioning, and tactics.

Organization

Teams play 8v8; each team attacks three goals and defends three goals. The field is 70 × 50 yards. The goals are 3 yards wide and are marked with cones.

Procedure

Teams play 8v8 and attempt to score on the opposing goals. To score, players must keep shots on goal below knee height. No corner kicks are allowed. When a corner is won, that team restarts the game from its back line. If the ball goes over the sideline, a throw-in is taken to restart play.

Key Points

- Stay compact and together when defending, and move the ball from side to side when attacking.
- Know when to pressure the ball and when to drop off, when defending.
- Communicate with your teammates.

Variations

1. Add one or two neutral players, so that the defending team is at a disadvantage and must focus on keeping its shape.
2. Each player has a two-touch maximum when in possession. On an interception, players are allowed three touches.
3. Each player has a one-touch maximum when in possession. On an interception, players are allowed two touches.

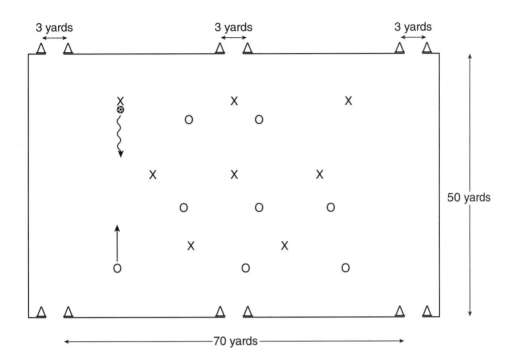

Purpose

Improve the ability to retain possession of the ball.

Organization

Form two teams of five, with two neutral players. Players are in a 30- × 40-yard grid. Place extra balls around the outside of the grid.

Procedure

Teams play 5v5, with two neutral players on the team in possession, and attempt to connect seven passes in a row to score a point. The first team to get 2 points wins the game; the first team to win three games wins the series.

Key Points

- When your team is in possession, make the field as large as possible by spreading out.
- Move off the ball to support teammates.
- Play away from pressure.
- Use a short-short-long passing pattern to draw the defending team in and then expose open space.
- Communicate with your teammates.

Variations

1. Each player has a two-touch maximum when in possession. On an interception, players are allowed three touches.
2. Each player has a one-touch maximum when in possession. On an interception, players are allowed two touches.
3. Vary the number of consecutive passes needed for a point.
4. Condense or expand the size of the grid to make it more difficult, or easier, to connect passes.

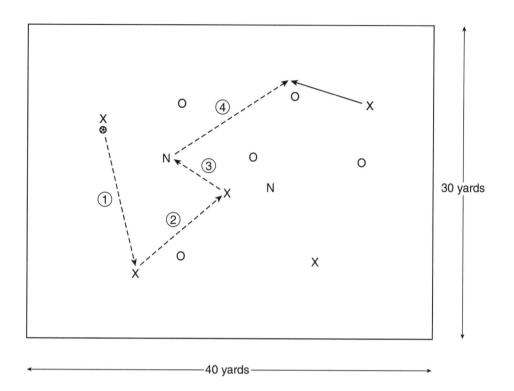

Purpose

Improve a team's ability to connect passes in a directional format.

Organization

Create a 40- × 60-yard grid, and place extra soccer balls on each sideline to restart play quickly if the ball goes out of bounds.

Procedure

1. Players (O_T and X_T) from each team stand on each end line and act as targets for their team.
2. The remaining five players from each team, plus one neutral player, attempt to pass the ball from end to end, using their target players for support if necessary, three times in a row. Example: Team A passes the ball to Target 1, then gets the ball back from Target 1, passes the ball amongst themselves in order to get it to Target 2, passes to Target 2, gets the ball back from Target 2, then passes again amongst themselves and eventually get it back to Target 1 for a point.
3. When an inside player passes the ball to a target player, the inside player replaces the target player. The target player then joins the inside players by dribbling the ball back into the grid.
4. The team in possession then attempts to get the ball to the target player on the opposite side.
5. Getting the ball from target to target three times in a row without losing possession equals a point.
6. The first team to score 3 points wins the game.

Key Points

- When in possession of the ball, look for targets first.
- Move as a group to support target players.
- Use a short-short-long pattern to draw the defending team in and then expose open space.
- Overhit long, flighted passes.

Variations

1. Each player has a two-touch maximum when in possession. On an interception, players are allowed three touches.
2. Each player has a one-touch maximum when in possession. On an interception, players are allowed two touches.
3. Each player must take a minimum of three touches to keep the ball moving.

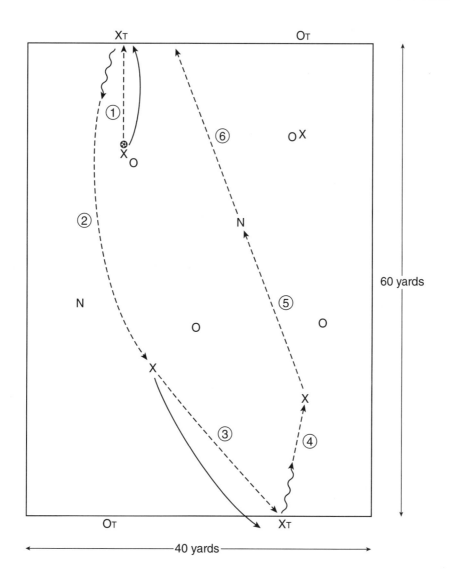

57   4V4 SQUARE POSSESSION WITH BUMPERS

Purpose
Improve combination play and transitions.

Organization
Teams play 4v4 inside a 20- × 20-yard grid. One neutral player plays on each side of the grid. Place extra balls around the outside of the grid so that play can be restarted quickly when the ball goes out of bounds.

Procedure
Teams play 4v4 inside the grid. The team in possession attempts to connect seven consecutive passes to score a point. The team in possession can pass to outside bumpers for support. Bumpers are allowed one touch only. Players play two-minute rounds and then rotate players in the middle and the outside. The first team to score 3 points wins the game; the first team to win three games wins the series (a).

Key Points
- Move to support the player in possession quickly, and as the ball is traveling.
- When your team is defending, stay compact and seal off one side of the field when possible. Press the ball quickly and together.
- Use bumper players to get out of tight spots.
- Receive the ball across the body.
- Know where the next pass should go.

Variations
1. Make the grid 15 × 15 and have players play 2v2, rather than 4v4, in the center. Have them play one-minute rounds. Five passes equal a point (b).
2. Make the grid 10 × 10 and have players play 1v1 in the center for one-minute rounds. Five passes equal a point.

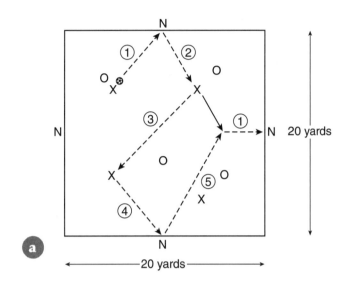

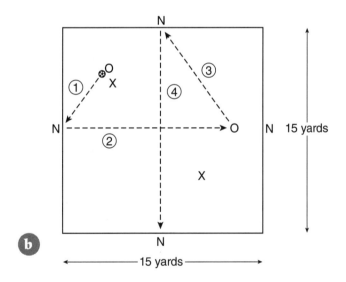

Purpose

Improve a team's ability to switch the ball from side to side quickly while retaining possession of the ball.

Organization

Split half a field, or a 60- × 75-yard zone, into four equal zones. Place extra soccer balls outside the grid so that play can be restarted quickly when the ball goes out of bounds.

Procedure

Teams play 8v8 (+2) possession inside the main grid. Players are free to move into any zone in the grid. Teams attempt to connect 10 consecutive passes to score a point. They can make no more than four passes within any zone. The first team to score 2 points wins the game; first team to win three games wins the series (a).

Key Points

- Move quickly to support the player with the ball.
- When your team is in possession, spread out so that not all players are in one zone.

- The team in possession must have a deep outlet in a different zone.
- Use a short-short-long passing pattern when in possession.
- Move the ball quickly in the tight space of a zone.
- Use driven or flighted balls to make big switches.

Variations

1. Split the grid into six zones, rather than four, and allow only three passes within one zone (b).
2. Each player has a two-touch maximum when in possession. On an interception, players are allowed three touches.
3. Each player has a one-touch maximum when in possession. On an interception, players are allowed two touches.
4. Each player must take a minimum of three touches to keep the ball moving.

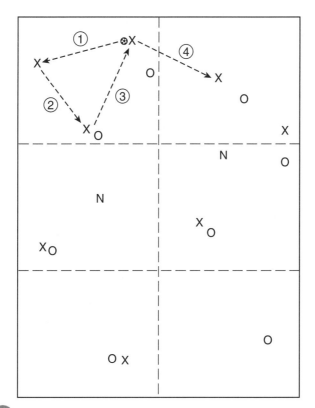

b

Purpose

Improve a team's ability to move the ball quickly.

Organization

Divide a 20- × 45-yard grid into three equal zones. Divide players into three equal teams and position them in the three zones. Stand with soccer balls outside the center of the grid.

Procedure

1. Serve the ball into team X's zone.
2. Team O sends two defenders into team X's zone to attempt to steal the ball or knock it out.
3. Team X attempts to connect five passes and then passes the ball into team Z's zone.
4. The O players in the center can block passes to other zones.
5. If the Xs switch the ball into team Z's zone, they win a point, and the Os send the middle players into team Z's zone to defend. The original defending Os return to the center. The Zs try to connect five passes and switch the ball back to team X's zone.
6. If the Xs are unsuccessful, and the Os steal the ball, serve a new ball into team Z's zone. The Os move into team X's zone, and the Xs send two defending players into team Z's zone and two into the center zone.
7. The first team to score 3 points wins the game (a).

Key Points

- Move the ball quickly between players.
- Weight passes appropriately.
- Overhit switch passes.

Variations

1. Each player has a two-touch maximum when in possession. On an interception, players are allowed three touches.
2. Each player has a one-touch maximum when in possession. On an interception, players are allowed two touches.
3. Increase or decrease the number of consecutive passes needed to switch the ball (b).
4. Make zones larger or smaller to decrease or increase the time and space when in possession.

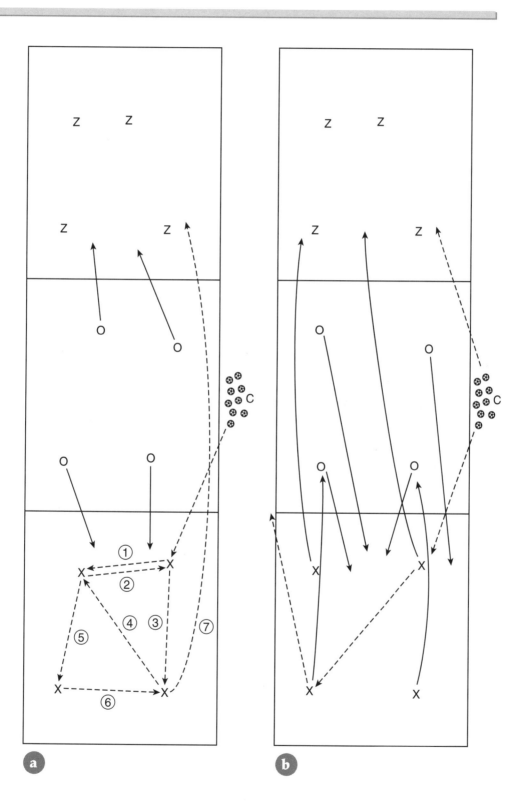

PASSING GATES

Purpose

Improve a team's ability to move the ball and defend as a group.

Organization

Randomly place 3-yard goals, marked by cones, throughout the inside of a 40- × 40-yard grid. Place extra soccer balls around the outside of the grid so that play can be restarted quickly when the ball goes out of bounds.

Procedure

Teams play 8v8 (+2) possession inside the grid. To score a point, a player must pass the ball through a goal to a teammate. Teams cannot score on the same goal twice in a row. The first team to score 10 points wins the game; the first team to win two games wins the series.

Key Points

- Move the ball quickly from side to side.
- When your team is defending, stay compact and together.
- Use a short-short-long passing pattern when possible.

Variations

1. Each player has a two-touch maximum when in possession. On an interception, players are allowed three touches.
2. Each player has a one-touch maximum when in possession. On an interception, players are allowed two touches.
3. Each player must take a minimum of three touches to keep the ball moving.

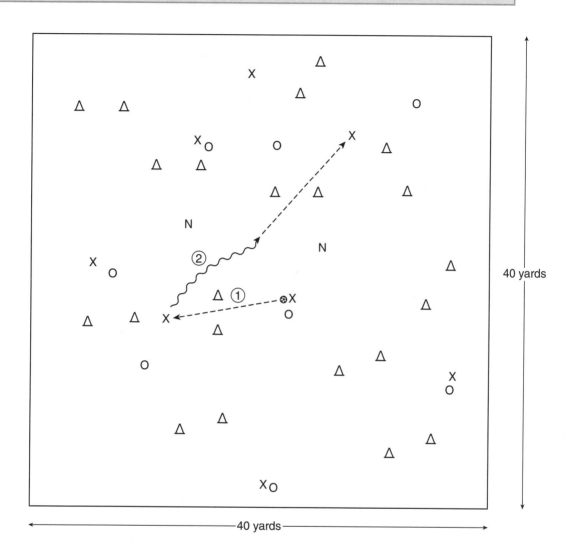

40 yards

40 yards

Purpose

Improve a team's ability to possess and move the ball quickly.

Organization

Teams play 6v6 (+2) in a 30- × 50-yard grid. Place extra soccer balls around the outside of the grid so that play can be restarted quickly when the ball goes out of bounds.

Procedure

Teams play 6v6 (+2) possession inside the grid. The team in possession attempts to move the ball from one target to the other, and then back to the first target, without losing possession. A point is scored by successfully moving the ball back and forth, without losing possession, three times. The first team to 3 points wins the game; the first team to win two games wins the series (a).

Key Points

- Look for target players (longer passes) first; play short only if a target is not an option.
- Move the ball quickly through the middle of the grid.
- Use a short-short-long passing sequence when possible.

Variations

1. After playing to a target, teams must connect five passes through the center before playing to the other target. This helps to establish a rhythm in possession (b).
2. Each player has a two-touch maximum when in possession. On an interception, players are allowed three touches.
3. Each player has a one-touch maximum when in possession. On an interception, players are allowed two touches.
4. Each player must take a minimum of three touches to keep the ball moving.

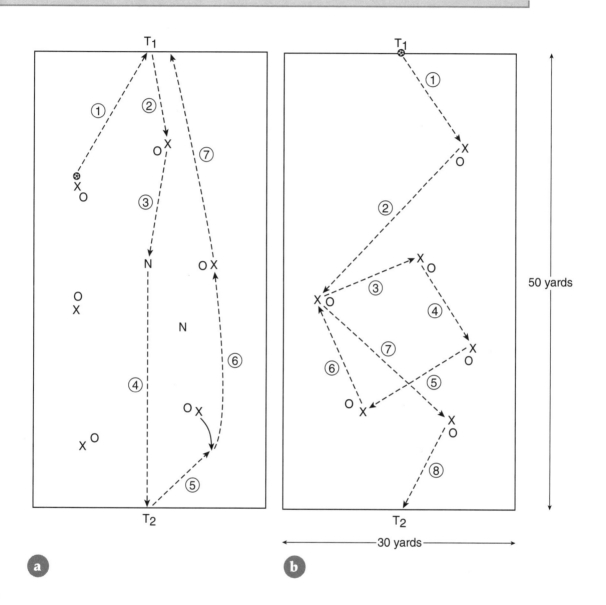

50 yards

30 yards

a

b

ATTACK! DEFEND!

Purpose

Improve transition, defending ability, attacking ability, and finishing.

Organization

Place two goals 50 yards apart. Mark sidelines 30 yards wide. Players form two teams, X and O. Xs form a line at each post of goal 1, with balls at one post. Os do the same at the opposite goal.

Procedure

On your command, the first O in each line attacks the first X in each line (2v2). Os attempt to score; Xs attempt to stop them. After a goal, an attempt on goal, or a steal by the Xs, the next two Xs in line immediately attack the Os that just attacked. The first team to score 10 goals wins (a).

Key Points

- Attack with speed. Make angled runs and overlaps, not just straight downfield runs.
- Transition from attack to defense as quickly as possible.

Variations

1. Teams place one line of players at the goalpost and the other on the opposite sideline, halfway up the field, allowing for an outlet upfield for a quicker attack (b).
2. Players play 3v3 rather than 2v2.

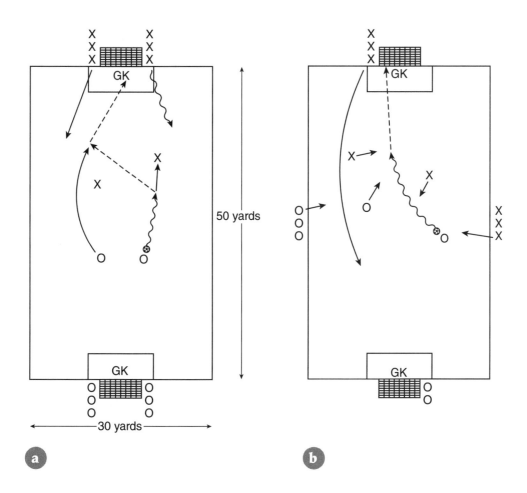

Purpose

Improve combination play and small-group defending.

Organization

Organize 12 players into two teams of 6. Mark a 20- × 30-yard grid, with a 3-yard-wide goal at each end. Each team places two players in the grid, two on the sidelines, and one on each side of its goal. Place extra soccer balls behind each goal.

Procedure

Teams play 2v2 in the center of the grid and attempt to score on the other team's goal. Players are allowed to pass to any bumper, on either team, for support or to combine. Bumpers are neutral when they are on the outside, but are part of their own teams once rotated onto the field. Bumper players have one touch. Players rotate after each goal, or after 45 seconds. For the rotation, inside players go to the sidelines, sideline players move to the end line, and end line players move into the field. After a goal is scored, the two players on the end line of the team that scored start a new ball (make it, take it) and attack two new defending players from the opposite team's end line.

Key Points

- Know where the next pass should go.
- Use the bumper players when possible.
- Play quickly in transition.
- Close down passing lanes when defending.
- Press the ball quickly; when defending, make players in possession put their heads down.

Variations

1. With additional players, play 3v3 in the center.
2. With fewer players, play 1v1 in the center.

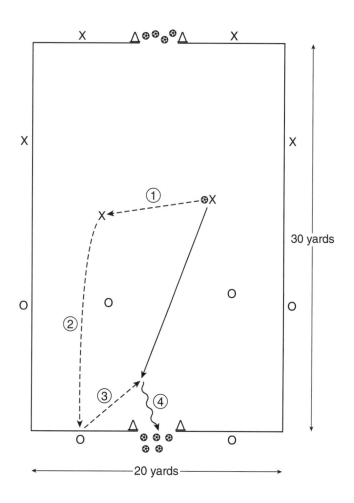

30 yards

20 yards

FOUR CORNERS 2V2

Purpose

Improve attacking, finishing, and small-group defending.

Organization

Place two goals 50 yards apart. Mark sidelines 30 yards wide. Stand in the center of one sideline with extra soccer balls next to you. Teams form two lines each, one at each corner of the field.

Procedure

Start the game by playing a ball into the grid. The first player from each line runs onto the field, making it a 2v2 situation. Each team of two attempts to score on the opposing team's goal. Start a new ball when a goal is scored or the ball goes out of bounds.

Key Points

- Attack quickly.
- Press the ball quickly when defending.
- Force the play to one side when defending.

Variation

The first two players from each line join play, making the game 4v4 rather than 2v2.

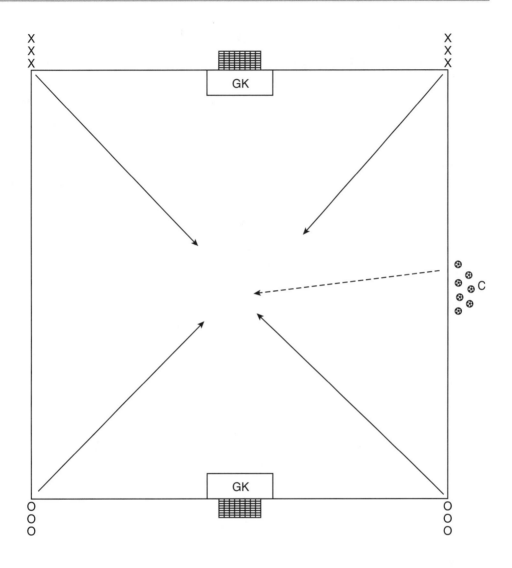

65   TWO ZONE OVER THE BORDER

Purpose
Improve the ability to retain possession of the ball, and improve the ability to defend in small numbers as a group.

Organization
Mark a 50- × 20-yard grid, with a center line splitting the grid in half. Split players into two teams of four. Stand at the center line with extra soccer balls.

Procedure
The teams start out in opposite halves of the field. Start the game by playing a ball to team X's side. Team O sends three players into team X's zone to defend. The Xs attempt to connect seven consecutive passes to score a point, while the Os attempt to either knock the ball out of bounds or steal it and return it to the remaining player on their side. The team in possession can use the entire grid (both zones), but has a numerical advantage only in its own zone. The defending team can send only three players into the opposite zone to defend. Teams play two-minute rounds. The first team to 3 points wins the game; the first team to win two games wins the series.

Key Points
- Move the ball quickly.
- Know where the next pass should go.
- Use open space to stretch out the defending team.
- When defending, work as a group, press together.
- Make the player in possession play short passes and squeeze the field with each pass.
- Make players in possession put their heads down.

Variations
1. Each player has a two-touch maximum when in possession. On an interception, players are allowed three touches.
2. Each player has a one-touch maximum when in possession. On an interception, players are allowed two touches.
3. Increase or decrease the number of passes needed to score a point.

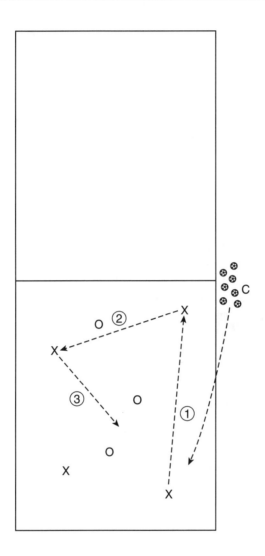

6V6 (+6) TO GOAL

Purpose

Improve all-around attacking and defending.

Organization

Place two goals 36 yards apart and mark a 44-yard-wide sideline. Divide players into three teams of six players. Two teams play 6v6 on the field, while the remaining six position themselves as bumpers around the outside of the field, one player on each sideline and one next to each post. The bumper players have one touch and play for whichever team has the ball. Place extra soccer balls in each goal so that play can be restarted quickly when the ball goes out of bounds.

Procedure

Start play by serving a ball into the grid. Teams attempt to score on goal. The first goal ends the game; the scoring team stays on the field and the losing team becomes the outside players. Allow no corner kicks; if a corner is won, the ball starts from the goalkeeper of the team that won the corner. Three corners won equals a goal. Bumper players are allowed only one touch.

Key Points

- Move as a group when defending.
- Play in combination when possible to create scoring chances.
- Always look for scoring opportunities.

Variations

1. Each player has a one-touch maximum when in possession. On an interception, players are allowed two touches.
2. Each player has a two-touch maximum when in possession. On an interception, players are allowed three touches.

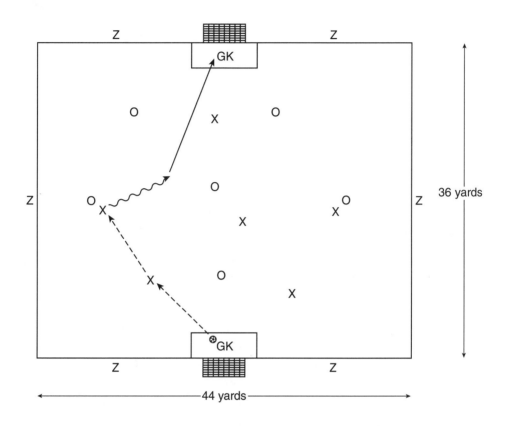

chapter 8

Crossing and Finishing

Crossing and finishing are both, in large part, technical actions. As with any technique, development occurs mainly through repetition. At first, give your players simple repetitions with rehearsed situations and pressure coming only from performing the technique correctly. Then, as they become more competent, increase the pressure by adding opponents, time constraints, and competition within the team during training activities. At the AS Monaco FC Academy in France, the youth teams conduct crossing and finishing training three times per week. In each of the 75-minute sessions, every activity is to goal. That repetition is necessary for creating top-level strikers.

Crossing

Accurate crossing allows a team and individual players to expose opponents' weaknesses as well as create dangerous situations that result in scoring opportunities. Many people think of crossing as simply a wide player serving the ball into the box from somewhere around the corner of the field. However, effective crossing comes in many forms: flighted crosses, near- and far-post crosses, cutbacks, early crosses, deep crosses, crossing on the run, and slip crosses, to name a few.

To improve the quality of their crosses, players must rehearse each one on a regular basis in functional, game-specific situations. When performing the crossing actions within each activity, players should focus on staying calm and controlling their bodies as they strike the ball. Balance is critical to crossing technique.

Players should also have a purpose when crossing. That is, they should have a specific idea of where they want the ball to go. The touch-look-cross pattern is a good way to get players in the habit of having a purpose. The "look" step in the pattern is critical. After the player takes her last touch, she either physically looks up or uses her peripheral vision to take a mental snapshot of the players inside the box. She uses the mental snapshot to determine the most effective spot for the cross.

Near-Post Cross With the near-post cross, the ball is served in the air or on the ground to the near post of the goal for an attacker to strike on goal, flick to a deeper spot in the box, or dummy for another attacker to strike on goal. Near-post crosses are most effective when an attacker in the box is on the run and can beat the defender or goalkeeper to the ball.

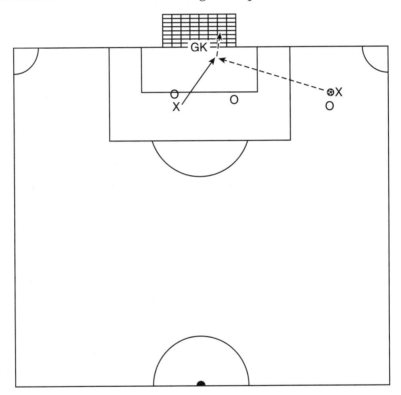

Near-post cross.

Far-Post Cross With the far-post cross, the ball is served, mainly in the air, to the back-post area of the penalty box after an attacker has either pulled away from his marker or is arriving late to the box, or after one or more attackers have made runs to the middle and near post of the goal. An effective far-post cross puts the ball where defenders in the middle and at the near post cannot get to it and where the goalkeeper cannot come out to catch or punch it.

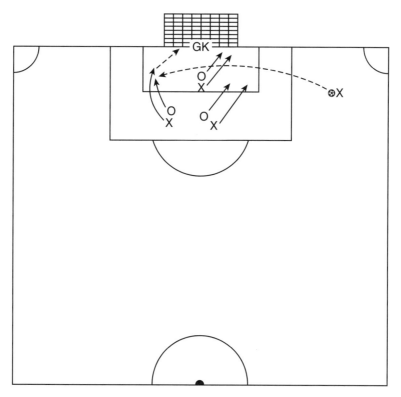

Far-post cross.

Cutback Cross   The cutback cross is done mainly inside the penalty box, when the attacker finds himself, through dribbling or a pass, at the end line of the field and behind the back line of the defending team. The attacker with the ball draws defenders toward him and cuts the ball back, on the ground or in the air, to the center of the goal for another attacker to strike. The cutback is effective because it draws the goalkeeper and defenders away from the center of the goal and forces the defenders to turn their backs on the attackers they are marking to watch the ball.

Crossing Behind the Back Line   Another effective form of crossing is achieved when the ball is served early, from a deeper position, into the space behind the defending team's back line. The cross is usually an outswinging or a whipped cross, or both, spinning away from the goal and toward the oncoming attacker. This type of cross is performed to expose the dangerous space between the defending team's back line and the goal. Similar to the cutback, a quality cross behind the back line gives an advantage to the central attacking players because the defenders who are marking them must first turn, or run backward, to defend the open space. That split second when the defender has to turn allows the attacker to get to the ball first.

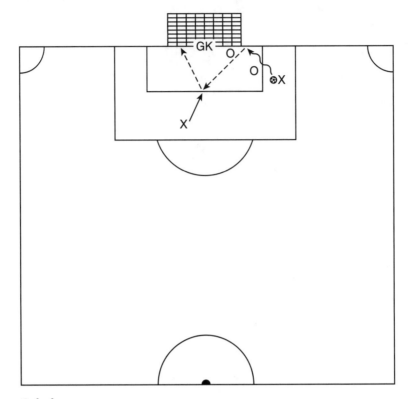

Cutback cross.

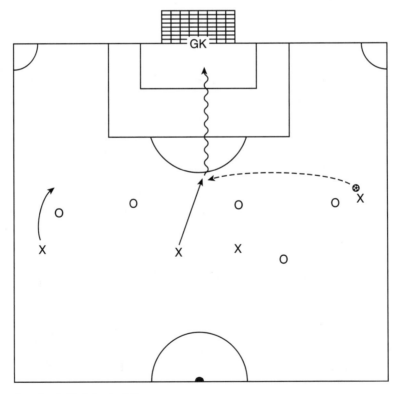

Crossing behind the back line.

Finishing

Like crossing, finishing is a technique that is developed through continual repetition. Some people believe that great goal scorers have an innate gift that cannot be taught; others believe that great goal scoring can be taught. What cannot be argued, however, is that to develop and refine finishing ability, players must continually be put in finishing situations that replicate those found in the game.

Finishing can take many forms. Shooting off the dribble, one-touch finishing, two-touch finishing, volleys, side volleys, bicycle kicks, and headers are but a few of the varieties. Good goal scorers use just about every part of their bodies to put the ball in the net.

Proper foot placement in relation to ball position is critical to successful finishing.

The moments before a goal-scoring opportunity are often the most frantic. On both sides of the ball, when close to the goal, players have a heightened sense of urgency, which can sometimes cause panic. The game can seem to speed up. Top-level finishers are calm and balanced; for them, the game seems to slow down and defenders seem to be in slow motion at the critical moment.

Good finishers also have the ability to time their runs into the penalty box in a way that allows them to arrive at the ball before the defenders or goalkeeper. The most effective finishers are active, which makes it easier to adjust to the position of the ball. Players should time their runs into the box so that they are arriving as the ball arrives. If a player runs into the box and then has to stop and wait for the ball, chances are that a defender will beat her to the ball. A player arriving at speed as the ball arrives is very difficult to defend.

Some scoring opportunities call for the ball to be placed, or passed, into a specific area of the goal, whereas others call for the ball to be shot, with power, at the goal. Both can be equally exploited; a player's choice depends on his ability to process the variables and his mental snapshot of the players in front of him. Generally the closer a player is to the goal, the more likely he is to go for accuracy rather than power.

A good finisher can strike the ball at a variety of angles and heights.

Other variables, such as the positioning of the goalkeeper, the angle of the shot, the player's control of the ball, the player's balance, and pressure from defenders also factor into the decision of what finishing technique to use. Training activities in which players are given a variety of goal-scoring situations will help players become more comfortable and confident when finishing.

Purpose

Improve shooting technique and accuracy from long range.

Organization

Set two goals 36 yards apart. Each player has a ball. Players form two lines at opposite goals. Place a cone in the middle (18 yards from each goal) for players to use as a reference.

Procedure

At the same time, players X and O dribble toward opposite goals and shoot as they approach the halfway point (top of the box), as shown in the diagram. Both players follow their shots for rebounds, collect their balls, and switch lines.

Key Points

- Use peripheral vision to note the goalkeeper's position and use it to decide between accuracy and power.
- Strike through the center of the ball with the laces.
- Toes should be pointed down, and the knee should come up during the follow-through.

Variations

1. The second players in line (X2 and O2) pass their balls out in front for the first players in line (X1 and O1) to run to and shoot.

2. Players X2 and O2 throw their balls out in front for players X1 and O1 to either control and shoot, or shoot off the volley.

3. Players X1 and O1 run, without balls, toward the opposite goals. Players X2 and O2 pass their balls out in front of the goals for players X1 and O1 to finish with one touch.

4. Players X2 and O2 throw their balls in the air for players X1 and O1 to volley.

5. Players X2 and O2 throw their balls for players X1 and O1 to head on goal.

6. Players X1 and O1 start in the center with their backs to the opposite goals. Players X2 and O2 pass their balls out for players X1 and O1 to control, turn, and shoot.

7. Players X2 and O2 throw their balls so players X1 and O1 must take them out of the air.

8. Make any of the activities competitive by setting a time limit and having each team count its goals.

9. Game within the game: Each player matches up with a partner in the opposite line and competes against that player in addition to competing as a group against the opposite line.

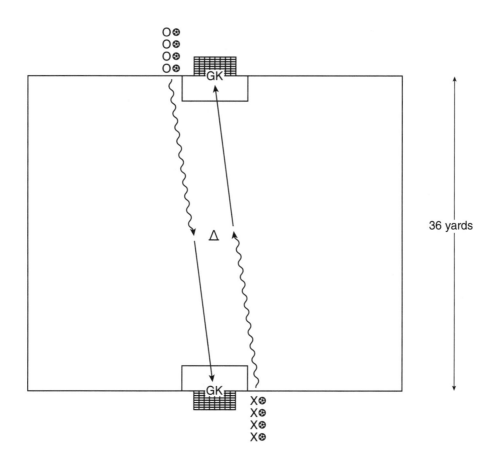

TWO-GOAL FINISHING

Purpose

Improve ability to shoot while running with the ball.

Organization

Set two goals 36 yards apart. Each player has a ball. Players form two lines midway between the two goals, on opposite sides.

Procedure

At the same time, players X1 and O1 dribble toward their goals and shoot as they reach the center. Both players follow their shots for rebounds, collect their balls, and switch lines (*a*).

Key Points

- Use peripheral vision to note the goalkeeper's position and use it to decide between accuracy and power.
- Run straight on before shooting; do not use a bent run.
- Strike through the center of the ball with the laces, or the top of the foot.
- Land on the kicking foot.
- Toes should be pointed down, and the knee should come up during the follow-through.

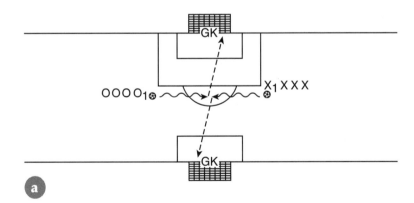

Variations

1. Players X2 and O2 pass their balls out in front for players X1 and O1 to run onto and shoot *(b)*.

2. Players X2 and O2 throw their balls out in front for players X1 and O1 to either control and shoot, or shoot off the volley.

3. Players X1 and O1 run, without balls, across the goal. Players X2 and O2 pass their balls out in front of the goals for players X1 and O1 to finish with one touch.

4. Players X2 and O2 throw their ball in the air for players X1 and O1 to volley.

5. Players X1 and O1 start in the center, with their backs to the opposite goals. Players X2 and O2 pass their balls out for players X1 and O1 to control, turn, and shoot.

6. Players X2 and O2 throw their balls so players X1 and O1 must take them out of the air.

7. Make any of the activities competitive by setting a time limit and having each team count its goals.

8. Game within the game: Each player matches up with a partner in the opposite line and competes against that player in addition to competing as a group against the opposite line.

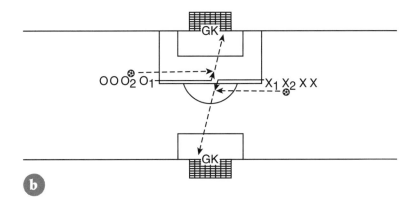

b

Purpose

Improve shooting and finishing technique from open play, while under pressure from a defender.

Organization

Set two goals 30 to 36 yards apart (depending on the ability of your players). Mark a halfway line. Place extra balls in the goals. Teams A and B have three players in their defending half, and one player in their attacking half (3v1 in each half). No player from either team can cross the halfway line. Team C stands behind each of the goals to retrieve balls.

Procedure

Play starts with the goalkeeper from team A passing the ball to a teammate. Team A moves the ball around its half to create a shooting opportunity. Play is live, so player B can steal the ball and score *(a)*.

Key Points

- No player from either team can cross the halfway line.
- A shot resulting in a corner kick restarts from the goalkeeper of the team that won the corner kick.

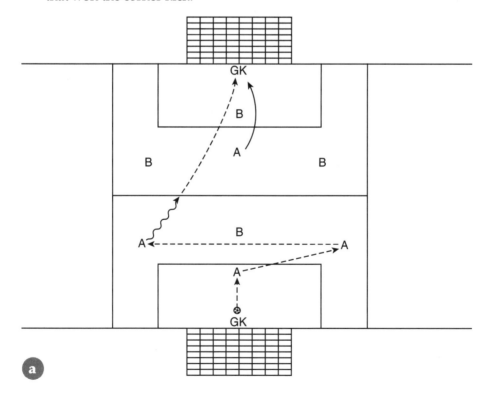

- Teams rotate each time a goal is scored (i.e., score to keep the field).
- Teams can pass to their player across the halfway line, using them for quick combinations when creating a scoring opportunity.
- Use peripheral vision to note the goalkeeper's position and use it to decide between accuracy and power.
- Land on the kicking foot.
- Toes should be pointed down, and the knee should come up during the follow-through.
- Follow all shots.

Variations

1. Players play one-touch, except for attacking-half players A and B, who have unlimited touches.
2. When attacking, one player can cross the halfway line by dribbling or to combine with attacking-half players A or B (b).

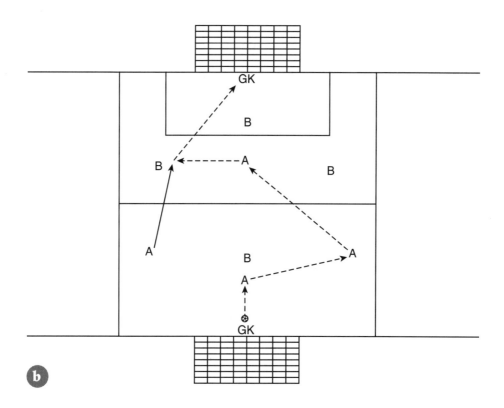

Purpose

To improve close range, reaction type finishing.

Organization

Set two goals 18 yards apart. The field is the size of the penalty box. Mark out two channels on the outside of the box. Create two teams of six, each with two players in the box, two on the end line of the attacking goal, and one on each sideline.

Procedure

Players play 2v2 inside the box. Outside (bumper) players have two touches to cross the ball from the sides and keep it in play on the end lines. Players play two-minute intervals and then rotate positions *(a)*. (Note: A bumper player is a neutral player who stays on the outside of the grid and acts as a wall, or bumper, to keep the ball in play.)

Key Points

- Have an attacking mentality, looking to score at every moment.
- Position so that crosses can be attacked.
- Follow all shots.
- Drive crosses to the near post and chip crosses to the far post. A driven cross is a line drive, fast-moving cross. A chip is a lofted, slower-moving cross.

Variations

1. Reshape the sidelines so that outside players can dribble toward the near post. Balls crossed from the end lines should now be cutback on the ground *(b)*.
2. Outside players can defend each other once they have received a pass.
3. Make the activity competitive by keeping an aggregate team score.
4. Game within the game: Each pair matches up with a pair from the opposite team and competes against that pair, in addition to competing as a group against the opposite team.

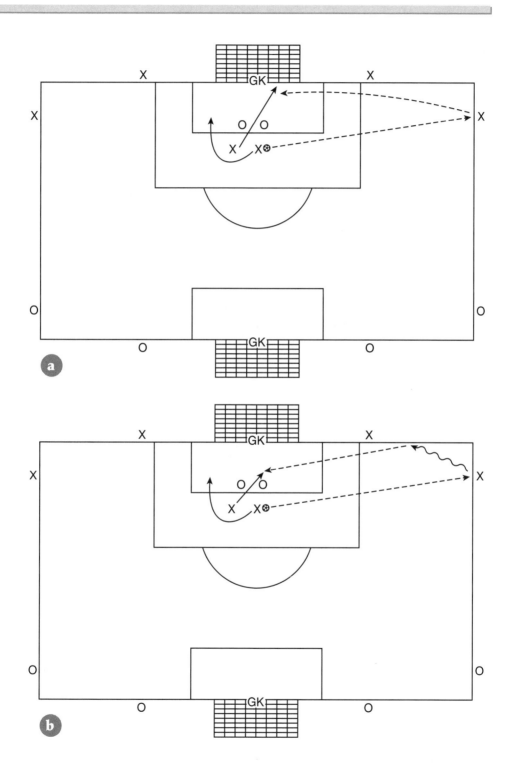

Purpose

Improve shooting and finishing technique and accuracy.

Organization

The field is the penalty box. Two players from each team are in the center of the box; all additional players surround the penalty area and act as bumpers for their team. Serve balls into play from the top of the box.

Procedure

Players play 2v2 inside the box. Outside (bumper) players have one touch to keep the ball in play. Serve the ball into the box to start game; then serve a new ball each time a goal is scored or the ball goes out of play. Players play one-minute intervals and then rotate positions (a).

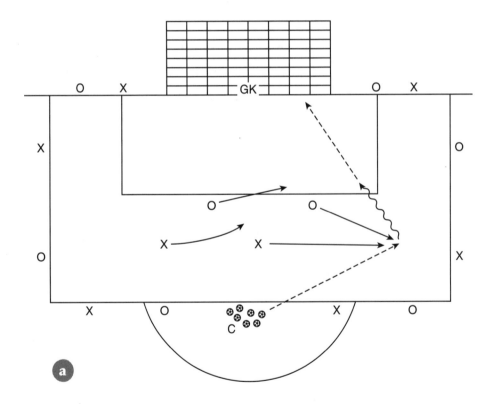

Key Points

- Have an attacking mentality, looking to score at every moment.
- Use peripheral vision to take mental snapshots of the goalkeeper's position.
- Follow all shots.

Variation

Outside players can join the play by dribbling into the box when passed the ball *(b)*.

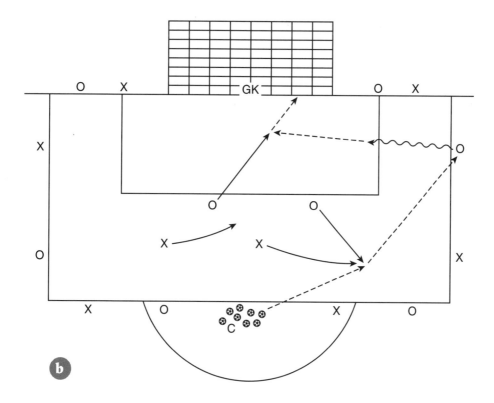

72

2V2 (+1) SERVING IN THE BOX

Purpose

Improve close range shooting and finishing, from balls served into the box.

Organization

Set two goals 18 yards apart. The field is the size of the penalty box. Place servers, with soccer balls, at each corner of the box. Two players from each team, plus one neutral player, are inside the box.

Procedure

Players play 2v2 (+1) inside the box. Call out a server number. That server crosses the ball into the box for both teams to attempt to score. Players play two-minute intervals (*a*).

Key Points

- Have an attacking mentality, looking to score at every moment.
- Position so that crosses can be attacked.
- Follow all shots.
- Drive crosses to the near post and chip crosses to the far post.

Variation

Use only one goal so that one team is attacking and one is defending (*b*).

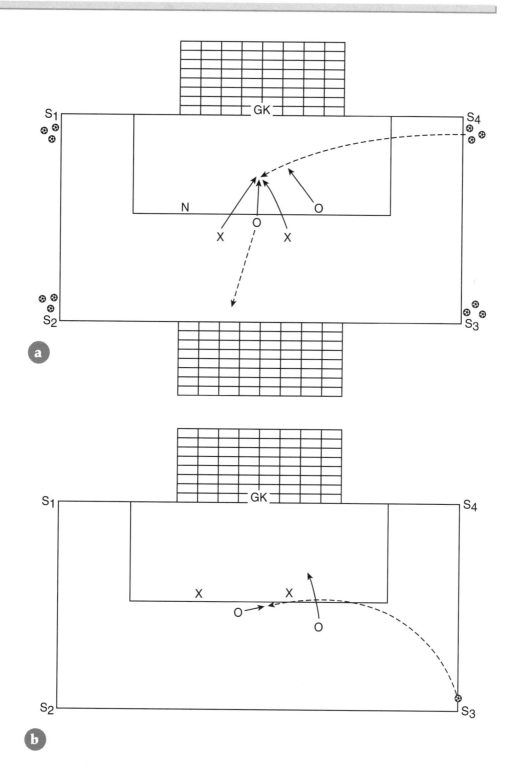

73

4V4 WITH WINGERS

Purpose

Improve shooting and finishing from open play

Organization

Create a 50- × 40-yard field with a goal on each end line. Players play 4v4 inside the field, with each team having a free wide player on each side of its attacking half.

Procedure

Players play 4v4 inside the box. Neutral players have two touches and look to cross each time they receive the ball. Neutral players cannot defend each other. Players play four-minute intervals and then rotate positions (a).

Key Points

- Have an attacking mentality, looking to score at every moment.
- Position so that crosses can be attacked.
- Follow all shots.
- Drive crosses to the near post and chip crosses to the far post.

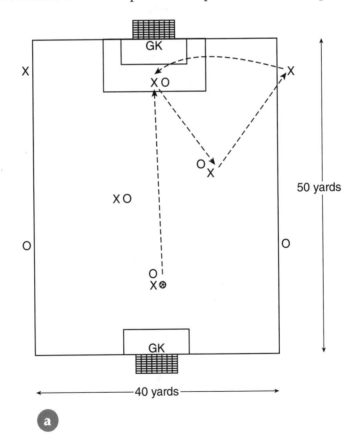

50 yards

40 yards

(a)

Variations

1. Reshape the sidelines so that outside players can dribble toward the near post. Balls crossed from the end lines should now be cutback on the ground.

2. Outside players have unlimited touches and must start in their attacking half, but can defend each other once they have received a pass.

3. One inside player can overlap the neutral player on the outside, making a 2v1 situation on the outside *(b)*.

4. Make the activity competitive by keeping an aggregate team score.

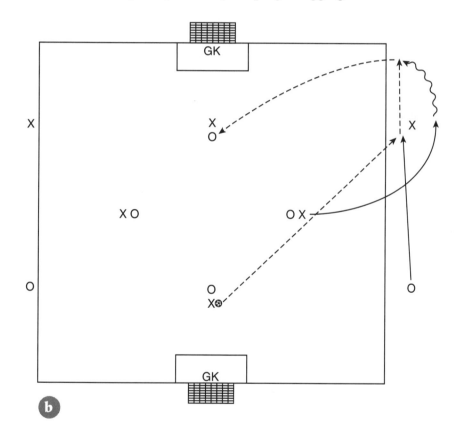

Purpose

Improve crossing and finishing technique and accuracy.

Organization

Create a field that is double the size of the penalty box, and set one goal on each end line. Two players from each team start in the playing area. Teams form two lines each at opposite ends of the field. Balls start at opposite corners.

Procedure

Players A1 and A2 attack goal 1 to start. Players B1 and B2 attack goal 2 to start. At the same time, players A3 and B3 pass balls to players A4 and B4 and follow their passes. Players A4 and B4 lay the balls off for players A3 and B3 to serve into the box. Players A1 and B1 and players A2 and B2 make near- and far-post runs, respectively, and attempt to finish the cross. Inside players run toward the opposite goals to receive the next cross. Players play one-minute intervals (a).

Key Points

- Drive crosses to the near post and chip crosses to the far post.
- Concentrate on making solid contact with the ball when finishing.
- Time runs so that you arrive as the ball arrives.

Variation

Player A3 passes the ball to player A4 and then overlaps player A4 so that the ball is moving away from player A3 before the cross (b).

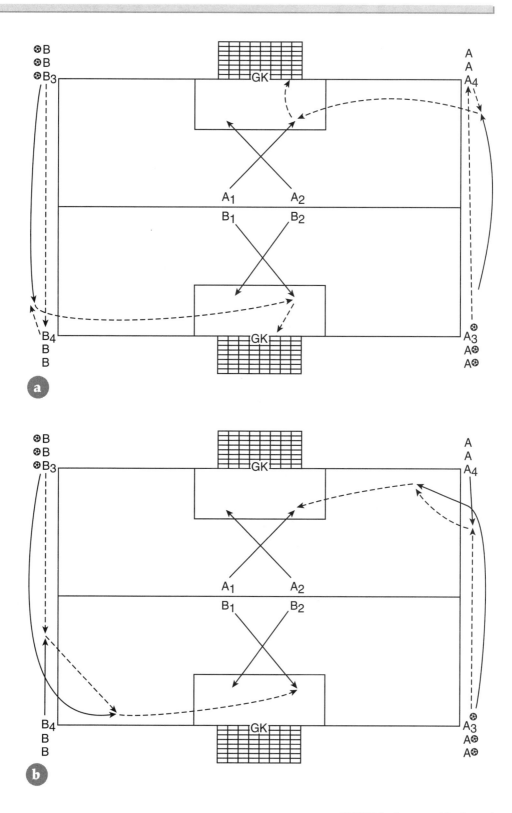

Purpose

Improve crossing technique and accuracy, and finishing technique and accuracy around the penalty box.

Organization

The field is the penalty box. Two servers are positioned outside the box. Two players start at the top of the box.

Procedure

Player X1 plays the ball out to player S1 (server 1), who dribbles the ball to the end line and crosses. Players X2 and X3 make near- and far-post runs, respectively, and attempt to finish the cross. Players repeat from the other side once the ball is out of play (a).

Key Points

- Position so that crosses can be attacked.
- Follow all shots.
- Drive crosses to the near post and chip crosses to the far post.
- When crossing, turn your hips so that they are facing where the cross will go.

Variations

1. Player S1 dribbles to the end line, toward the near post, so that the cross is cut back on the ground or chipped to the far post (b).

2. Player X1 plays the ball out in front of player S1, so that player S1 is running to the ball when crossing.

3. Player S1 is positioned so that the cross is coming from a deep position. Player X1 lays the ball off for player S1 to serve with one touch.

4. Player S1 is positioned so that the cross is coming from near the corner flag. The cross should be driven to the near post.

5. Player S1 is positioned so that the cross is coming from wide of the penalty area and on the ground behind the back line of the opposing team. Player X1 plays the ball to player S1, who controls it and then plays it on the ground in front of players X2 and X3.

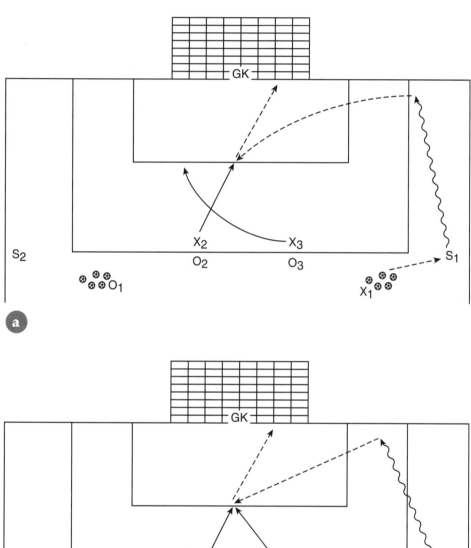

chapter 9

Conditioning

Soccer players need technical ability, tactical understanding, and mental toughness in order to succeed. At the highest levels, soccer-specific conditioning and fitness are also crucial to players' ability on the field. Without a high level of conditioning, players will inevitably fall short in match situations.

A famous, and somewhat controversial, example of a team's conditioning program is from the 2006 World Cup. Jurgen Klinsmann, the German national team coach, gave each of his players a conditioning program to follow in the year leading into the World Cup. Each player had his own program to follow, which was specific to that player's position and optimal fitness level. The fitness program was successful: The German team took third place, losing to eventual world champion, Italy, in the semifinals. The program was controversial in Germany, however, because Klinsmann used American fitness experts to develop the program.

General Soccer Endurance

General soccer endurance can be described as a player's ability to deal with the varied intensity of a match. A soccer player covers a distance of 3 to 6 miles (about 5 to 10 km) during the course of an average soccer match, during which the player may be sprinting, jogging, or walking. A high level of general endurance helps players deal with fatigue and allows them to exert optimal effort throughout a match.

Interval training is the most common method of improving players' endurance. It includes both a work and a rest period. During the work period, the player reaches 80 to 95 percent maximum heart rate, and during the rest period the player recovers to approximately 20 percent maximum heart rate.

The ratio of work to rest is the critical component when working to improve soccer fitness. When a player is just beginning to train, a work-to-rest ratio of 1:3 may be appropriate. For example, a player may work for 15 seconds and rest for 45 seconds, then repeat the exercise. As the player becomes more physically fit, the ratio may be lowered to 1:2 or 1:1.

During rest periods, players should carry out some form of light, soccer-related activity, and not simply come to a complete stop. For example, they may juggle individually or pass with partners during the rest period.

Effective interval training will improve players' ability to recover quickly from periods of high intensity, allowing them to be more effective during a match.

Complete Soccer Fitness

In addition to training for endurance with cardiorespiratory training, top-level players must also condition a variety of other athletic attributes, such as flexibility, agility, balance, speed, strength, and power. Teams and coaches often use agility and flexibility exercises as warm-ups or cool-downs during training. This helps the players prepare or recover, as well as improve their conditioning.

Flexibility

The ability to conduct movements with an appropriate range of motion determines a player's flexibility. The two most common methods of increasing flexibility are static stretching (standing toe touches) and dynamic stretching (lunges). Static stretching is commonly used for general flexibility, whereas dynamic stretching can be used for soccer-specific movements.

Increasing flexibility helps players perform technical actions more efficiently and also aids in injury prevention. With a high level of flexibility, players are less prone to soft tissue injuries such as muscle pulls and joint sprains.

Agility

Agility can be defined as a player's ability to change direction quickly and easily. For soccer purposes, a player should work to improve the ability to change direction both with and without the ball. Incorporating an agility ladder, juggling routine, and fast footwork into training can help to improve agility. Dribbling a ball through cones set up in a slalom formation, for example, or moving without a ball through an agility ladder with both feet touching inside each block can help improve agility.

When performing agility ladder work, it is important to allow enough distance between players to prevent interference.

Balance

Top-level players have the ability to maintain balance while running with and without the ball, before and after jumping, and most important, when being challenged or challenging for the ball. Small-sided games, circuit training, and agility ladders in training provide a variety of situations and repetitions that improve balance.

Speed

Soccer-specific speed is more than just the ability to cover distance in a short time. Although covering distance quickly is crucial, the ability to cover the distance with and without the ball, manipulate the ball quickly, and process information and take action quickly are also important. Improving speed is difficult and generally is done through exercise repetition and small-sided games.

Training Methods

Conditioning can be improved in a variety of ways. Basic training can include running and sprinting over a distance, both with and without the ball, and stretching—both static and dynamic. High-intensity small-sided games allow players to work at a high rate for a limited time and then rest. Circuit training, in which players rotate through a variety of conditioning stations, is also a good way to improve players' conditioning.

Because as a coach you have a limited time with players, training must be as economical as possible. Using activities that improve conditioning as well as technical and tactical ability allows players to improve greatly in a shorter time. Small-sided games are a great way to train economically.

Following is an example of how exercises from this book can be combined to create training sessions:

Warm-up: speed, agility, and coordination circuit (see chapter 2)

Speed, agility, and coordination exercises (chapter 2): Acceleration; Agility Ladder Work; Agility Running

Passing and receiving exercises (chapter 5): Groups of Four; Four-Point Passing

Attacking and defending exercise (chapter 7): 4v4 Square Possession With Bumpers

Crossing and finishing exercises (chapter 8): Two-Goal Finishing; 2v2 to Two Goals

Conditioning exercises (chapter 9): Group Sprints; 300-Yard Shuttle Run; 1v1 Keep-Away

Purpose

Test and improve general fitness level.

Organization

Use an athletic track or full-size soccer field.

Procedure

Players should jog and stretch before undertaking the test. Players complete eight full laps (2 miles, or 3.2 km) around the track, without stopping. Record the finishing times for all players. The standard time for elite players to complete the full eight laps is 12 minutes.

Key Point

Maintain a steady pace throughout the run.

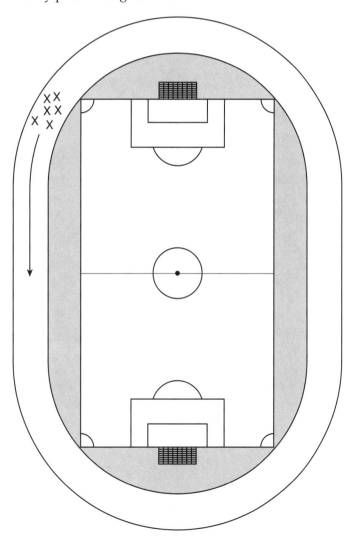

Purpose

Test and improve the overall fitness level of elite players.

Organization

One full-size field. Set up the course as shown in the diagram.

Procedure

On your signal, players complete four consecutive laps around the course in 12 minutes, as follows:

1. Run forward to the first flag at the half line.
2. Run backward to the next flag at the top of the penalty box.
3. Run forward to the center circle cones.
4. In the center circle, run forward throughout. Run to the center cone, out to the left, back to the center cone, forward to the top cone, back to center, out to the right, back to center, back to the starting cone.
5. Run forward to the next flag, at the top corner of the field.
6. After rounding the flag, run forward across the half line, doing a 360-degree spin at each of the cones along the way.
7. Slalom through the flags.
8. Run forward to the corner flag.
9. Shuffle sideways facing the course to the flag at the top of the box.
10. Shuffle sideways facing away from the course to the flag in the corner.
11. Run forward jumping as if shooting a header at each of the three cones along the way.
12. Run forward through the starting point.

Key Point

Maintain a steady pace throughout.

Variations

1. Players complete one lap as fast as they can, rest for one minute, then repeat, for a total of four runs.
2. Set up the course on a half field; players should complete four laps in six minutes on the shortened field.

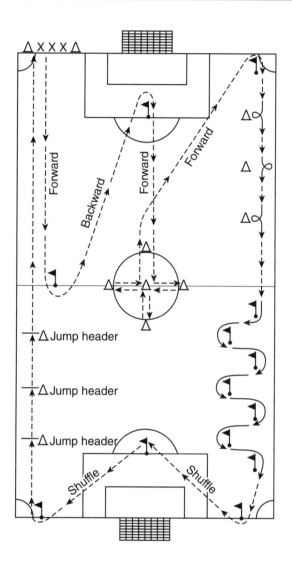

△ X X X △

Forward

Backward

Forward

Forward

△○
△
△○

↑△ Jump header

↑△ Jump header

↑△ Jump header

Shuffle

Shuffle

Purpose

Improve anaerobic conditioning.

Organization

Mark two lines, 60 yards apart. Separate team into three groups, 1, 2, and 3. Group 1 starts on line A, group 2 starts on line B, and group 3 starts behind group 1 at line A.

Procedure

On your signal, the following occurs:

1. Group 1 sprints across to line B.
2. When the last player from group 1 crosses line B, group 2 sprints across to line A.
3. When the last player from group 2 crosses line A, group 3 sprints across to line B.
4. When the last player from group 3 crosses line B, group 1 sprints back across to line A.
5. Groups continue until each group has completed 10 sprints across.
6. Players rest for two minutes. Mark two lines 20 yards apart.
7. Have groups repeat the procedure until each group has completed 15 sprints across.
8. Players rest for two minutes. Mark two lines 10 yards apart.
9. Have groups repeat the procedure until each group has completed 20 sprints across.

Key Points

- Sprint through each line.
- Encourage your teammates throughout.

Variations

1. Increase or decrease the line distance.
2. Increase or decrease the number of sprints each player must complete.

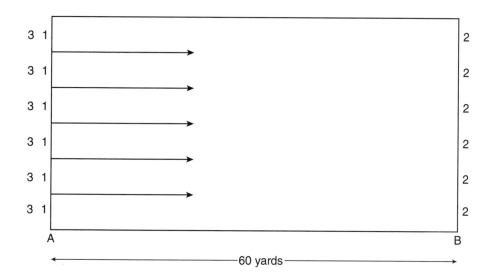

Purpose

Test and improve the anaerobic fitness levels of elite players.

Organization

Mark a starting line and place cones at 10-, 20-, 30-, 40-, and 50-yard intervals.

Procedure

On your command, players sprint:

1. Out to the 10-yard marker and back
2. Out to the 20-yard marker and back
3. Out to the 30-yard marker and back
4. Out to the 40-yard marker and back
5. Out to the 50-yard marker and back

Players should complete the run in approximately 45 seconds. Players complete five runs, resting for one minute between runs.

Key Points

- Maintain a high sprint pace throughout.
- Control your breathing, stand upright, and continue moving during rest intervals.
- Encourage your teammates throughout the run.

Variations

1. Increase or decrease the number of total sprints.
2. Increase or decrease the amount of rest time between sprints.
3. Have players juggle during their rest times.

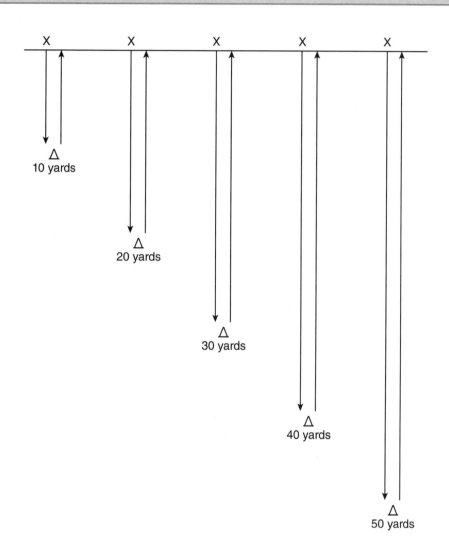

Purpose

Improve anaerobic fitness level and recovery time.

Organization

One full-size field (120 yards long), or a field space 120 yards long.

Procedure

Players start on the end line. On your signal, they have 15 seconds to sprint to the other end line. Players then have 45 seconds to jog back to the starting line. Have them continue until they have completed 10 sprints and 10 jogs in 10 minutes.

Key Points

- Control breathing when jogging.
- Encourage teammates throughout the run.

Variations

1. Increase or decrease the number of sprints.
2. Increase the amount of time players have to sprint from one end to the other.
3. Increase the recovery run time.

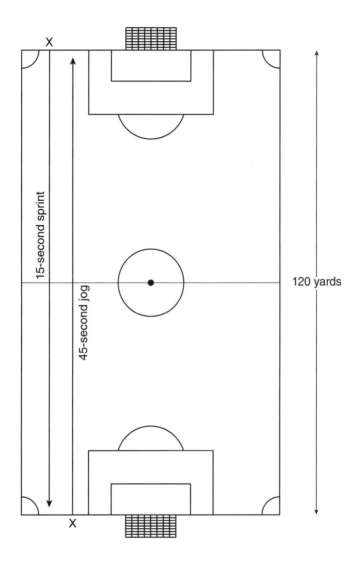

Purpose

Improve overall fitness with the ball.

Organization

Mark a 30- × 30-yard grid. In the grid, players get into pairs, with one ball between them.

Procedure

On your signal, each pair plays 1v1 Keep-Away within the grid. Players attempt to steal from their partners and retain possession. Pairs play for one-minute intervals and then rest and switch partners. Players play 10 rounds.

Key Point

Recover when in possession of the ball.

Variations

1. Pairs play for 30-second intervals.
2. Players have a 30-second rest and recovery time.
3. Players play for five rounds.

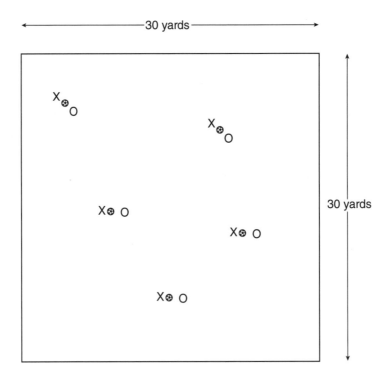

Purpose

Improve recovery time and overall conditioning.

Organization

Mark two lines, 60 yards apart. Players start on line A.

Procedure

On your command, players sprint to line B and back to line A in 15 seconds. Players then rest for 30 seconds, repeat the sprint, and rest again, continuing until they have completed eight runs.

Key Point

Control your breathing during recovery.

Variations

1. Increase sprint time to 20 seconds.
2. Increase recovery time to one minute.
3. Increase or decrease total runs to make the exercise more or less demanding.

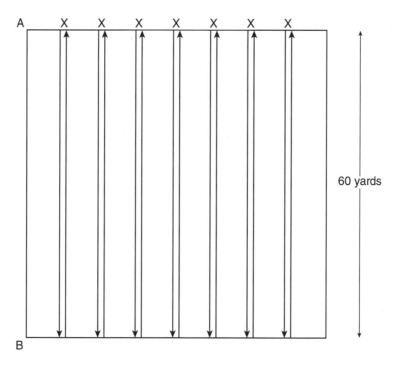

FARTLEK RUNS

Purpose
Improve general and anaerobic endurance.

Organization
Players use a full-size soccer field or an open area.

Procedure
Players jog for 10 minutes to warm up and then do the following on your command:

1. Jog for 60 seconds.
2. Run at three-quarter pace for 90 seconds.
3. Jog for 45 seconds.
4. Sprint for 10 seconds.
5. Jog for 30 seconds.
6. Run backward for 30 seconds.
7. Walk for 30 seconds.
8. Run at three-quarter pace for 60 seconds.

Have players repeat the sequence four times.

Key Points
- Control your breathing throughout.
- Encourage your teammates throughout.

Variations
1. Increase or decrease the amount of time each step is performed.
2. Increase or decrease the number of repetitions.

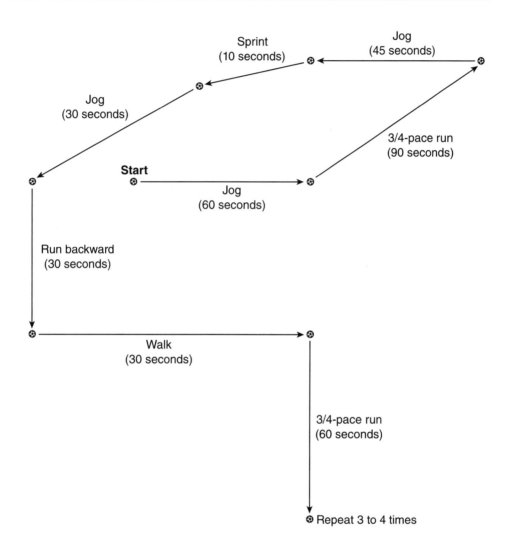

Sprint
(10 seconds)

Jog
(45 seconds)

Jog
(30 seconds)

3/4-pace run
(90 seconds)

Start

Jog
(60 seconds)

Run backward
(30 seconds)

Walk
(30 seconds)

3/4-pace run
(60 seconds)

⊗ Repeat 3 to 4 times

About the Authors

Mike Matkovich joined the coaching staff of Chivas USA as the assistant coach in February 2008. A veteran of American soccer and founder of Chicago Magic soccer club, one of the most successful youth soccer clubs in the United States, Matkovich has coached at every level of the U.S. game, working with youth, high school, college, amateur, and professional teams.

Before joining Chivas USA, Matkovich served as an assistant coach for Toronto FC, an MLS team, during the team's inaugural campaign in Major League Soccer in 2007. Earlier, Matkovich served as director of Chicago Magic for 17 years. Under his tutelage the Magic was named *Soccer America*'s No. 1 Boys Club in the nation in 2004, 2005, and 2006. While with the Magic, Matkovich was named National Coach of the Year and Regional Coach of the Year by the National Soccer Coaches Association of America, and the Illinois Coach of the Year by the Illinois Youth Soccer Association. Matkovich also served as an assistant coach of the Chicago Power of the indoor National Professional Soccer League from 1990 to 1994, where he won a national championship in 1990. He spent 2000 to 2006 at the helm of the Chicago Fire reserves of the Premier Development League, where he amassed a 71-8-7 record, which gave him the highest winning percentage of any coach in PDL history. A member of the U.S. national coaching staff, Matkovich holds a national A license from the USSF and has been a member of the NSCAA since 1992.

After a standout youth soccer career, **Jason Davis** helped the University of Akron win three conference championships. After college, Jason played professionally for the Pittsburgh Stingers, Detroit Neon, and Detroit Safari of the Continental Indoor Soccer League (CISL). While playing professionally, he began coaching local youth teams and decided to pursue coaching as a full-time career. Davis has coached at the club level for the Michigan Wolves-Hawks, Michigan Metrostars, and Vardar soccer clubs. He has also served as the director for the Michigan Metrostars and the Vardar Boys and Vardar Academy. He holds a USSF A license as well as the USSF national youth license and is a state and regional head coach for Michigan and the Region 2 Olympic development program.

You'll find other outstanding soccer resources at

http://soccer.humankinetics.com

In the U.S. call 1-800-747-4457

Australia 08 8372 0999 • Canada 1-800-465-7301
Europe +44 (0) 113 255 5665 • New Zealand 0064 9 448 1207

HUMAN KINETICS
The Premier Publisher for Sports & Fitness
P.O. Box 5076 • Champaign, IL 61825-5076 USA